To- Melis[illegible]
Brando[illegible]

Babies' Guide to Parents

Enjoy the journey!

(and other important people)

Love you guys!!
Congratulations!
YoYo

Babies' Guide to Parents
(and other important people)

Just Believe Publishing ©

Book Design by Bruno Ferarri @ Pillow Design©
Author's Front Cover photo by Heartfelt Photography©
Design Layout by Meri Ramey-Gray

Published in the United States of America

ISBN:978-0-6152-1857-1

I loving thank all of the many people for their kindness and support without whom I would have not completed this endeavor of love. With all my heart,thank you!

Preface

Hey, to all parents, young and old
if you are going to be having one of us (a baby),
or you are thinking about it and what it entails,
then you definitely need to read this book.
This is all about 'Babyhood' (a.k.a. 'Parenthood') .
This book will reveal clues about us,
also hints and facts to help us all get along!
Hopefully, you (parents, guardians, grandparents, etc.)
will feel good with the guide book that we
(general population of all babies)
have given to you. Please, feel free to reflect back to
the book if a tough situation comes up.
We can only recommend to keep this guide book
handy at all times for best use.
Good luck!
Let the adventure begin!

Table of Contents

Chapter One

We're Coming!!

Did you just take a test and find out that at least one of us is on the way? We don't know how you feel, but right now, we are a little bubbly. We do hope that you are expecting us, or are at the least, excited and surprised. Excitement helps to bring patience in the long run. If neither of the above applies to you, and you feel positive about our upcoming appearance, we welcome you to feel free to read our guide book. You will do a great job!

Most importantly, make sure that you find a good doctor! This person could be the first person to hold us. If you don't like him/her, we will know. Every time you go into one of those 'doctor visits', and there is a big ball being rolled over our head, and you are growling under your breath, we know! All the squishing, kneading, poking, and prodding is very unnerving, so for both of our sakes, pick the right doctor.

Each doctor visit is supposed to keep you posted on how well we are doing, growing, and developing. The most wonderful thing is to let you know that there is at least one of us growing inside of you. Generally, though, at most visits, it is not explained that while we are growing inside of you, we are listening to your heartbeat, voices, music, humming, whistling, your dreams, concerts and movies. Just as a hint, please go see whatever movies and concerts you can before we arrive because we will take up some of that leisure time.

It is also good to get exercise and eat a healthy diet. Take the required prenatal vitamins too, making sure that you get plenty of folic acid; we like that a lot. Stretching and walking are really good exercises; we get to relax to the soft beat of your steps. Never forget to get plenty of sleep because you will need it!

Also, in preparation for our arrival, pick baby items that you will need for us to spend time together, such as a glider or rocker, books, bassinet, crib, stroller and an appropriate car seat. (Very important! Car seats can usually be properly installed, often for free, at our friendly neighborhood fire or police department.) We know that crib bedding is very enticing with all the frills; however, we can smother ourselves in all of the extra material. Please, keep bedding to a minimum and stuffed animals in their own spaces.

Just as a note, we know that our bedroom gets painted and decorated, but make sure that the paint is okay to use because the fumes can be harmful to us. We personally recommend a paint that has no VOCs! VOCs are the chemicals that emit from the paint itself, and long after it has been put on the wall. One more thing, color of a room can dictate emotion. Please, do not paint our room all in black or another really dark color. These darkening colors can effect us in ways where we are not lively, not quick to smile, or we do not want to grow and develop because we do not see a shiny future surrounding us. We like bright and lively color around us! As a side note, it would be good to be proactive and get a paint that is washable or, wallpaper is easy to scrub on, too. Thanks for paying such close attention!

Please, refrain from use of illegal drugs, alcohol and smoking of any kind; this is most appreciated. The use of these items can have grave effects on our well being, even long after our arrival.

We do recognize your voice while we are growing

inside of you. We can also recognize daddy's voice, or whomever is with our mommy. Even though we are sleeping most of the time that we are in the womb, we are changing every day! And we are really looking forward to meeting you on our big day!

With the big day approaching, this is a great time to go over our list of necessities for you and for us. If there was a baby shower for our arrival, or you did all the shopping, this is the time to make sure that all of the bedding, receiving blankets, outfits, burp cloths and cloth diapers have been washed. Please wash all of our items in a baby detergent, such as Dreft™ or All™ Baby Wash. These detergents are specifically made for us with the sensitivity of our skin in mind.

Now, very important, let's go over the list of 'baby bare essentials'. Let us proceed with the following items:

*Baby nail clippers
*Infant pain reliever
*Infant ibuprofen
(for fever reducer)
*Q-tips / Rubbing Alcohol

*Diapers
*Baby Wipes
*Infant gas drops
(pass gas)
*Baby bath wash / wash pad

*Onesies (lots!)

*Sleepers (lots of these, too)

*Vapor bath (for colds)

*Vaporizers (for colds, too)

*Pacifiers (age appropriate)

*Bottles and nipples

*Diaper rash cream

*Baby powder

*Receiving Blankets

*Burp cloths (plenty!)

(We would also like to recommend at this time that you get a breast pump for yourself, even a hand-held one, in case we are apart for too long so that you can relieve the pressure you will experience.) Also, in going through this list, double check for any manufacturer recalls and return those items immediately.

Well, we think that covers us for the next three months. Yes, three months! We would also like to explain the list in a little more detail, such as the diapers. Do not buy too many of one brand or make sure that they can be exchanged if they were a gift, because sometimes we can have a reaction to our diapers. It can take trying a few brands to see which ones we are comfortable with. This can be true with almost anything with which we can come into contact, including diaper rash ointment, formula, and detergent. Once we know what works, then that would be a good time to buy in bulk because we will use them all! However, going back to the list of essentials, feel comfortable in knowing that you have a good amount of items to care for many of our needs.

The only thing left that we will need, though it is never the least, is your unconditional love. Now, with that in mind, we will be seeing you real soon on our big day! We are so excited to meet you, we love you so much!

Chapter Two

The First Three Days

"Whoa! What is going on here?! I am upside-down (hopefully) and there is all this squeezing and pushing and squishing. Nobody told me about this part! Talk about a change of comfort zones. And, oh my gosh, that watery thing that I have been bouncing on has just popped and it disappeared! Out of nowhere, it just deflated. I don't get it. I am so confused. Ow! Am I getting pushed around here? Oh, yes I am. The walls around me are contracting and every time the walls come back in, I get bumped in a downward motion. I have no idea what is going on around here. I really hope that you do. I am just heading towards the light. Just so you know, this is a little scary for me and I hear you yelling and there are others around chanting, "Push, push!" Whoa, I am coming out somewhere and here is my debut!"

"AAAAAHHHHH!!!!!!!!!! AAAAAHHHHHH!!!!!!!!!!"

"What is going on here?! I am cold and there is this sticky, wet stuff all over me! And who are those ladies cramming stuff in my mouth? Oh, gag me! Not literally! Now they are in my nose and cleaning every orifice that I have. I had no idea all this was going to happen. Had I known, I would have stayed inside where it was warm and cuddly and I had all I could eat. Could you have warned me?"

"Oh, a blanket! Yes, nice and tightly wrapped up in this warm blanket. I love this. This is much better. Now, where am I going? I am being handed to a lady. Oh, I get it. You were the one who was carrying me this whole time. Wow, I grew inside of you and ended up here. I hope you are ready for this because I am totally lost! My world just turned upside down and I need you, Mommy, to help me get through all of this. Thank you in advance because I am so confused. I don't know what I would do without you." (This information is being provided to us by one of our own who felt comfortable about being interviewed about their experience. Thank you, Fred. We shall continue with his interview as long as he feels comfortable.)

“What are those flashes of light and all of these people holding me? I gather that this episode of my life will show up in a photo album at some time so that I may see this experience from a different view. That is all right, as long as I do not have to relive it. There is a band being snapped together on my wrist that looks like my mommy’s. Where did my mommy just go? I am put on some kind of cart that wheels through all these hallways and different rooms. Look at all the bright lights! My goodness! Now, we’ve stopped and there are some nice folks checking me and putting something on my wrist. My blanket has been taken off. Something is now being put on me to cover my bottom and other private areas down there. Interesting... I haven’t had anything like that on before either.”

“Whoa, I am being picked up and there is something covering my head. Now, my head is out. That’s good. This same thing is being pulled over my belly and my arms are being pulled through their own holes. Now, they are snapping this thing together in between my legs. It does seem pretty comfortable. However, I am being rewrapped in my blanket and all is well with the world. This is my favorite, so far. It reminds of where I just came from.” (This is a clue - snugly wrapped blankets help us to sleep and feel comforted, especially in the next few weeks.)

"Now, I get to see my mommy again! Yeah! Oh yes, I recognize your voice, heartbeat and warmth. I could just fall back asleep and dream away. What a great feeling to be in your loving arms!"

(We would like to take this time to again, thank Fred for all of the memories that he recalled, no matter how traumatic they were. Fred understood that it is for the greater good of all babies. If we could all be so brave; thanks again, Fred. We will help you from here on out.)

We think that we may start to become a little hungry. Of course, we are not sure how to go about doing this. At our old place, there was this tube that brought down this liquid, full of processed stuff that just filled our bellies. But, we don't have that here. So, how do we go about doing this? Let's see...... "MOMMY!!!! AAAAAHHHHH!!!!!!!!! We are hungry! Our belly is starting to hurt and we need some food! Can you help us? Oh, we feel so helpless!"

Okay, a different lady (lactating nurse) is walking into the room that we are in with our mommy. This lady is helping our mommy pull out her breast and is trying to put that in our mouth! How are we supposed to put that in our little mouths? How do we even open our mouth? The nurse is tickling the underneath of our chin and the side of our cheek. Apparently, our mouth opened up and that nurse put the nipple of the breast in our mouth. So, then we try to open our mouth, but we are sucking instead and now there seems to be a liquid coming out. Oh yeah, that tastes good, too. Ooh, and it is going down to our belly, right where we are hungry. This works great! This is what they call breast-feeding.

The nice lactating nurse is still with us and is telling our mommy all of the wonderful things that come with breast feeding. The nurse explains that the 'breast milk' that I am receiving is extremely important to have, especially in the first three days. In these first three days, the breast milk is not really milky at all, but it does contain collostrum. The collostrum has built-in immunities which we get directly from you to help us become healthy and strong. This is also how we receive natural defenses to help keep us from becoming sick. This is very good stuff! There are many vitamins and minerals in the breast milk that help to give us our good baby fat from which we grow big and strong without becoming over or under weight.

*Additional benefits of breast-feeding include:

-time we get to spend together	-milk is always warm
-sick less often	-diapers don't smell as bad
-all natural!!	-easier for us to digest
-less gas and spit-up	-less chance of allergies
-some say we're smarter for it	-helps you get back in shape
-it's free!	-readily available
-much less cleaning for you	-not over or underfed

-reduces your chance of breast cancer
-the most complete and balanced nutrition for us

If other family members would like to feed us, so that we can spend special time with them, then the breast milk can be pumped or a bottle of formula can be prepared. If we are a really hungry eater, you may need to supplement breast-feeding with a bottle of formula, especially until the breast milk comes in regularly and we have gotten on to a regular feeding schedule. (This can sometimes take a few weeks; you will feel the difference.)

Now, to help make sure that there is always milk readily available, it is necessary for you to drink LOTS of fluids;

especially water. Drinking lots of fluids reduces your chances of getting clogged milk ducts which are very painful. This is different from engorgement. With engorgement, the whole breast swells because the milk is not being released on its schedule. These situations usually subside with our feedings, pumping, hot shower, and with the help of a warm wash cloth, if you need it. Some say that placing a cabbage leaf inside your bra, while you are wearing it, naturally releases the pressure, too. Interesting, huh?

Feel free to ask the lactating nurse any and all questions that you may have about breast-feeding and breast milk. It is better to ask than to not have an answer. Also, if by chance the hospital or facility does not have a lactating nurse, ask for guidance or assistance to get all the information that you will need. The rewards are tremendous!

Now, moving to our diapers. That was the interesting item that was wrapped around our bottom area early after our arrival to keep us from going to the bathroom everywhere. Our first stools (doo-doo), are usually black and seemingly tar-like. This will happen until the breast milk comes in. We think that it also may be leftover from what we ate in the womb, since we no longer have anywhere to dispose of that either.

Diaper changing is a very important event. If you have any questions about this, again, please ask. We are all very lucky if a nurse comes home with us, but that is not generally the case. It is highly recommended to make sure we are thoroughly cleaned after each bowel movement; wiping from front to back. If we are not, then we are very susceptible to diaper rash and other infections. Believe us, we will let you know just how uncomfortable that is! Be prepared to change our diaper 6 -10 times per day following about 10 feedings per day. Sometimes we may need more, but never less.

For those of us who are boys, we are usually circumcised in the hospital about a day after we are born. Circumcision is a surgical procedure done on boys where the foreskin is removed from the tip of the penis exposing the hole that our urine comes from. It is up to our mommies and daddies to make this decision. But, like the lactating nurse, there will be someone at the hospital to help you make that decision. This person is our doctor, the pediatrician (infant and child physician) that you have picked for our care. However it may be someone else who performs the circumcision due to religious practices, or another staff member available at the hospital.

If you need more information with this decision, we

have made you a list of some pros and cons. We truly hope that this will help!

*Pros of Circumcision
-less likely to get urinary tract infection in the first year
-cancer of the penis is about 0% in circumcised males
-eliminates foreskin infection
-much easier to keep penis clean
-less bladder infections through and into adulthood
-prevents phimosis, a narrow opening that makes it impossible to retract the skin at a later age

*Cons of Circumcision
-risk of something going wrong with surgery, though it is slim
-circumcision might not heal correctly

We know that you will make the right choice, but it is best for us that you make the decision in the hospital, right after we are born. We hope that this added information is helpful to you.

Even if we are not boys, we do get a visit from our pediatrician in the hospital to look us over and to see that we are faring well. This information will also be included in our paperwork when we are released from the hospital.

On another note, we have our umbilical cords. They can look pretty gruesome. There are some resources that have umbilical cord banks. These are places that store our umbilical cords since they carry our DNA; if we would happen to need that resource later on in life. Our umbilical cord studs generally fall off about two weeks after we are born. Clean the umbilical stud with cotton swabs (such as Q-Tips® as the cotton would not have a tendency to pull on our scab) and rubbing alcohol to help dry it up in order for it to fall off, unless it gets a cut. If it does, do not put alcohol on the cut because it will really cause us pain!

Until then, be gentle when putting on our diapers. Try not to have the diaper rub on the cord because that is a bit uncomfortable. This can be relieved by folding down the front of the diaper; some newborn disposable diapers come with a semicircle cut out to make room for the umbilical cord stud. (Another hint; this type of diaper is much more comfortable and easy to use, especially if you do not feel like folding the down the top rim of the diaper.)

Non-disposable diapers are still used widely in the world. You just want to make sure that they have the thicker area down the middle to make sure that they absorb what they should be absorbing so that our excrement does not fall down our leg. Each time that you change one of these diapers, take it off immediately and wash it. If you want, shake some baby powder into the diaper to help chaffing from happening. (Chaffing can occur when wet material rubs against us for a period of time. This is why it's important to remove it as quickly as possible.) Plus, these diapers are eco-friendly, as they are reusable and do not pile up in a landfill. Another thing to note, that they are very cost effective when you are trying to watch your money.

Another big point to remember is, until our umbilical cord has fallen off and if we have been circumcised, it is better to give us dry baths until everything is healed. A soapy wash cloth wipe-down is just fine. When bathing us, make sure to hold us very secure or lay us on a mesh bath sling. Bathing information will be discussed further in the next chapter. If our umbilical cord stud does not fall off after three weeks, it is perfectly fine to ask the pediatrician to help remove it.

We believe that another item needs to be addressed in our arrival period and that is the shape of our heads. If we were born through a vaginal birth (meaning you pushed and we entered this world through the birth canal), our heads may be shaped a little funny. Some people refer to this as 'cone-shaped'. Surprisingly, this worries some mothers when they assume that we are born with a perfectly round head. This is not always the case. Sometimes forceps are used to help us come out, which may attribute to our funny head shape or just being squeezed out an opening the size of an almond could have done it. Either way this occurred, it is normal. Somebody figured out that this would happen to us, which is why we were given a soft skull with which we can also recover nicely. Thank God for whoever came up with the idea! (Pun intended.) Moving on.....

Our hospital 'first photo' is also taken within our first 48 hours here. It's a great little keepsake, especially when they are printed with our height and weight on the photos. How cute! It is also a wonderful idea to bring a special blanket or outfit for our first photo shoot!

We believe that all basic items have been addressed thus far. However, we cannot stress enough that if you have any questions, now is the time to ask them. Remember to take home doctors names and phone numbers, in case you think of anything later.

Just so you know, Mom, most mommies do not leave

the hospital with flat bellies (another little myth). This normally takes time to work-off, but guess what? We are going to help you with that since we kinda helped you to put that weight on. You have to admit, some of those cravings were delicious, weren't they? And sometimes, food didn't taste so good as did that second. We enjoyed those cravings, as well!

Chapter 3

Our First Month

What a wild ride, huh? Hopefully, we are entering our new home after having traveled from the hospital in our safely installed car seat. We cannot say for sure how you are doing, but we believe we are famished. You may have noticed on our way home we do have a tendency to relax and fall asleep to the soft rhythm of a vehicle. Do you know about those stories you hear where parents are giving us rides in the middle of the night to help us fall asleep? Totally true! A snug fit in our car seat gives us extra security.

Make sure that we are well 'swaddled' in our blanket. Often, a nurse will swaddle us before handing us to you right after our birth. (Swaddled refers to how we are wrapped in our blanket to remind us of being in the womb. Quick course on swaddling: lay us down on our blanket with our head close to one corner. Take the opposite corner where our feet are pointing to and pull that part up on top of us. Take the right side corner and bring it across our chest and belly and tuck it in under our backs. Next, pull the left side corner and wrap it around covering all the pieces you have laid and that corner would end up around our back. Make sure that it is a 'snug' fit. This is sometimes the only thing that we need to comfort us, plus, if you pick us up, too, that is an extra bonus.)

Thank goodness that we have all arrived home safely. Depending on our house size, there might be two bassinets for us, one on each floor, and a baby monitor next to each. Truth be told we are exhausted and you should be, as well. A good rule of thumb for this first month is to sleep when we do. The amount of rest you get is very important in order to be able to keep up with our disconcerting schedules. Having prepared for our arrival by purchasing our necessities and everything washed and ready to use, sleeping should be really easy.

If there are others in the house to help, great! If other people are able to bring over prepared meals, frozen or hot, it is all greatly appreciated. Forgo the general cleaning routine to enjoy some extra ZZs. Here's a tip, it's okay if visitors come by and the house is not spotless. You just had one of us and that is greater than any cleaning job performed. All of our visitors should appreciate this. Remember we feed off of you, literally. If you are upset, distraught or uncomfortable (even by the house's level of cleanliness), so are we! On that note, try to keep a special place where we can go together to have a calming period, whether to have a feeding or just rock gently. We will learn about this place very quickly.

Here is a special hint, do not eat pickles, broccoli, onions, green peppers, banana peppers or other gaseous foods while you are breast-feeding. We digest them through the milk and we will have a LOT of gas. Large amounts of gas is very painful to us and you will know by our screaming! To make this easier, try to steer clear of these gaseous items. If we do become uncomfortable from gas, move our legs like a bicycle to help push it out or use infant gas drops to help. Sometimes, we need both and that's okay. Thank you very much.

We need to explain to you what happens to us with visitors, *especially* in the first month. If any visitors come by who are sick, please ask them to come back when they are well. We do not have all the immunities we need to fight the many viruses out there. An important note if anyone has measles, do not let them in the house. This virus can be fatal when it is exposed to us until we receive our immunzation to it at twelve months old.

We do need to address an important issue about smoking. Of course, it is better to not smoke but if you need to, please make sure that all smoking is done outside of the house, this is greatly appreciated. Smoking inside the house can cause grave effects to our as well as your lungs, especially for those of us who were born early. If someone is ready to handle us who just had a cigarette, make sure they wash their hands and fingers with soap and water to scrub off the nicotine. It's also better to have a jacket on while someone is outside smoking, then they may take it off when they come in. This insures we do not receive a transfer of nicotine from the shirt being worn. These are very important tips where your efforts are greatly appreciated.

It is also a good idea to have some type of antibacterial foam or soap for visitors to cleanse their hands with prior to holding us. We love other little children such as our siblings or cousins who may wish to hold us. Please, do not just hand us off to little ones. They may be unable to understand that we are not dolls or toys and they may injure us. There must always be an adult supervising us.

Here is another important reason for writing this book. We want adults to understand where we come from (not the literal part), but why we do what we do and what causes us to react. With regards to visitors and outings, it has been found that we easily become 'over-stimulated', such as too many people coming to see us at the same time, music playing too loudly, or just too much going on. Well (Extremely Important Information Coming, Read Carefully!), we do become over-stimulated by many different means. If we have a visitor who is having a really bad day, don't pass us over to them. We will become scared by feeling how anxious they are, if they're sweating, yelling or the fact that their heartbeat has been heightened. We will feel this and become uncomfortable. (Our discomfort can usually be noted by our crying.) In addition, if you are having a bad day, just make sure that we are in a safe place, such as our crib or bassinet, and ask for help to make your day better. Do not let anyone who is having a bad day, take it out on us.

Another 'heightened' factor is that we do not have normal vision. We will not be able to see normally for about four to eight weeks. We are able to distinguish black, white, and red because of the significant contrast in the colors. We cannot really see anything past a distance of about eighteen inches. For this very reason, we use our other senses to help comfort us.

THIS IS A HUGE WAKE-UP CALL! We have grown to this point with a true understanding of our mother's heartbeat and what happens with our mother, such as her smell. Now that we have arrived, please understand we do not know who 'Grammy' is, and may not for some time. We know how our mother breathes, feels, speaks and smells. We become 'over-stimulated' by being introduced to a huge crowd of people wanting to touch and hold us. Each time we are passed on to the next visitor, that's one more person to smell their perspiration, deodorant, perfume, cologne, shampoo, hairspray, shower gel, body lotion and whatever else has been used in their daily routines. Do you know how you feel when you enter a perfume store, have smelled fifteen different perfumes, and then smelled coffee beans to clear your senses? That is what happens to us!! This is ONE source of our 'over-stimulation'. Our 'coffee bean' is our mommy, daddy, or whomever's smell is our main source of love.

Along with each person's smell, the environment smells different, too. A backyard barbecue, with the grill, is going to smell much different than the smell inside the house.

Among our heightened senses is our hearing. To us, each person sounds and talks differently. Sometimes, this can be very scary for us. Nothing personal, but we do not know who you are, though you may know us. Please, understand it takes time for us to get to know you and recognize your voice. Of course, the more you are around, the more we will get to know you. We have a very short-term memory and we will for a long time but we recognize smells, sounds and touches.

We generally respond well to soft-spoken voices, even if they are in a very deep tone. It is kind of funny, a long, deep tone is something we would recognize from our time in the womb. (Thanks, Daddy and Grandpa, for taking the time to talk to us before our arrival.) This usually gets our attention if we are crying and upset, definitely deterring us from further outbursts. In addition to our first meetings with new people, you must understand that while all of this extra sensing is going on and our schedules can easily be interrupted. We may not nap for quite some time due to our brains working overtime. Please note, we will eventually get our sleep.

This is a good time to take us to a restaurant while you

dine because this is something we handle pretty well. The many conversations that go on sound like muffled white noise. It is relaxing. For the most part, we will sleep through your entire meal. (This is a really neat hint!) The difference is the many people around us are just enjoying their meal. This is different than people who wish to hold and play with us, which can cause over-stimulation when we are their main focus of attention. So, as a good note, white noise is soothing. Some of our youngest newborns relax to soft music, a staticky radio station, television, a washer or dryer or even a vacuum. These are all muffled constant noises to us, just like being in the womb. Some mommies vacuum while we are sleeping; it's okay. We think that you are getting the gist of this enough to let us move to our next topic.

Our 'top-notch' research group came up with another important subject to address - temperature. This is not defined by us running a fever, but our core temperature. (Take note of this information.) If we are born in the winter and depending on our locality, it is important that our head and feet are covered. We need an undershirt to help keep our 'core' warm under our outfit. If we need coats or blankets, please, wrap us in them. An important message, if we are being transported in a vehicle and the heat is all the way up then we start to sweat. JUST LIKE YOU! This makes us very uncomfortable. Doing this consistently raises our core temperature, and we will always have to be bundled up this way. Keep us as covered as you are. It is a good idea to always have an extra blanket on hand in case the temperature outside drops. This also pertains to the hot months. If you guys are dressed in shorts and t-shirts, we should be, too. Please, do not bundle us and take us outside in the heat. Not only is it uncomfortable, but we get heat rashes and are more susceptible to heat exhaustion or heat stroke. Always take good note of the temperature outside and dress us accordingly. Hopefully, the temperature inside our house is around 70 degrees Fahrenheit, so we remain pretty comfortable.

Just to touch base quickly on our nighttime feedings, DO NOT LEAVE A BOTTLE IN OUR MOUTH WHEN WE GO TO SLEEP!! Okay, so it is a little more important than to just touch base on. Doing this leads to early tooth decay before we even get teeth! This is referred to sometimes as 'bottle rot'. Also, if we have a bottle in our mouth, and have a difficult time breathing for whatever reason, do you think that you will hear us? Most likely, the answer is no. If we start coughing, we could then start choking, and you may not have any idea that this is happening. Now, if we fall asleep with a bottle, or a breast in our mouth and then it is removed as soon as we fall asleep, that's okay. It is no longer in our mouth. See how that works? Easy enough, right? Like we said, this is a 'guide book' to make this whole experience safer and easier. You are doing great!

Our vision is something that we don't have much of right now. We see more shadows than regular movement. For this reason, some people purchase black and white colored mobiles or mobiles that have mirrors (a really cool one). We have a better chance of seeing the sharper contrasts. But do not feel offended if you are wondering why we may not look you in the eye, it's a little hard for us to find them. We will follow your voice and try to find the source. As weeks pass, our vision will become more clear.

As an overview from the beginning, we will be having our first check up this month. An infant pain reliever (acetominophen) is really good to off-set the pain received from our shots. If you remember to do this prior to our appointment, that would definitely help. Look at the box for the correct dosage amount. Sometimes the dosage goes by either age or weight. Normally, you want to go by our weight as it will be the most accurate dosage for us at this time. If you are unsure, call the doctor before the visit. If there are any other questions that you may have about our growth and development, make a list to bring with you. This is a good idea to follow for all of our visits.

Please keep us current with our shots. This will prevent us from getting ill. Our pediatricians will have a shot chart or booklet to update at each visit. If the cost of the shots is too high, ask our pediatrician if there is a public health center where shots can be given at little or no cost. Receiving our shots can mean life or death, so if necessary, ASK! This is that important!

Adjusting to us is a big change. We will learn about each other together. Sometimes we cry and we know it is hard for you to figure out why, but we can give you a few pointers. Make sure that our diapers are dry, bellies are full, our temperature is good and if we have passed gas. This passing gas thing can be a real chore. We must burp, good ones, after being fed. If not, then our stomachs get upset until we pass gas. Infant gas drops can help us to pass gas if needed. Some of us even finally let loose one big burp and fall right to sleep!

We will not be spoiled, contrary to big peoples' popular

belief, by being held or picked up each time we cry. Actually, it increases our self-esteem and confidence to know that we are loved so much that someone is willing to help us figure out what we need! Thank you so much!

Just as one little note, please use the infant fingernail clippers to trim our fingernails. We understand that our nails are soft and flexible. Try not trimming too close to our fingers to keep from cutting our skin or nail bed. We are sure you have noticed that we bring our fingers to our face often and have a tendency to scratch around our eyes and noses. This is why it is a good idea to keep our nails trimmed, especially the sharp corners.

There are times, once in a while with some of us, that we have been crying and you can't figure it out. You have gone through all of the regular reasons, they have been checked and the solutions are not working. Try to give us a gentle bath, sing to us softly, read anything, use a pacifier or take us for a drive in the car. If you feel that you cannot take our crying, DO NOT <u>EVER,</u> <u>EVER</u> SHAKE US! Under no circumstances! Again, put us in a safe place, like our bassinet or crib and go to another room and call a friend or read a chapter in a book. Calm yourself down before coming back to tend to us. It is okay to give yourself a break. We know we take up most of your time. If you ever feel overwhelmed, take a moment or ask for some help. We know we are not the easiest sometimes, but we do love you so much. We promise that it is all worth your while.

We need to be moved frequently from just laying on our backs. This can form a flat shape on the back of our heads. Pick us up and carry us with you or place us in a bouncer. The most important thing is we cannot consistently lay on our heads and we do appreciate your help with that matter.

Oh, okay. We just had a question raised. One parent just asked if one of us is just not happy being held by mommy, should the daddy intervene and hold the baby to comfort them? Absolutely! Sometimes, we just want to smell his mustiness and feel his strong arms. No one can just raise us all alone without any help from anyone. Plus, if there is more than one parent in our home, we need both of them equally. Some say that there is nothing greater in this world than the bond within a family, we happen to agree. It does take a village to raise a child.

Chapter 4

Month Two

Movin' on up! How are you doing? We are doing great! We are gaining weight and getting taller! Within the next week or so, we can show you our first real smile, while we are looking at you! How cool is that? We get to look up at you and show you our gummy grin! We should have worked ourselves into a better schedule. (By 'better schedule', we mean one that is more predictable). One thing that can be more predictable is if we have colic. A 'colic' episode, which consists of nonstop crying and can go for over an hour, usually occurs at the same time every day. If we do have colic, discuss it with our doctor. If you have not yet discussed it with the doctor, then please do. The doctor may have something to help us *all* get through this phase. The good part is that we grow out of our colic usually by the end of month three. There really is not a lot that you can do to help, so get a good book, a cup of tea and a safe place for us to be. It will soon be over.

Now, unless the doctor has told you otherwise, we are still being fed only breast milk and/or formula. It is necessary that you follow this guidance. Our tummies cannot digest other food items. Certainly not table food, nor pudding, especially rice pudding. Rice may tear our intestines right now, thus creating an extremely painful condition. This could possibly lead to further digestive problems down the line. Plus, dairy products can cause our bellies to possibly stop up, giving us constipation. The basic point is that we just cannot digest any of these things easily. This flows into a golden rule that if we are not happy, you are not happy. So please, please, do not give us anything else, no matter how tempting, even if 'grandma' says that it is okay.

Of course, no disrespect to grandmas as we do believe that there are many wonderful things they can share to help our new mommies and daddies adapt to us. We are thankful for our grandmas and their advice. *(Such as if we get the hiccups, wet our pacifiers with some water, no spit, and sprinkle a little sugar on it, so that we will continue to suck on it, making the hiccups go away. Thank you for this,

Grandmas, this is a good one!)

The tip of our umbilical stud has fallen off by now and has left us with a belly button! Wahoo! This means new baths! Also, if we had a circumcision, this should have cleared up as well and we are feeling great! No more worries as to whether the diaper is going to rub the wrong way, or having to make sure that each spot was cleaned very carefully. Regular diapers and baths from here on out! Now we may be bathed in a kitchen sink or in our own separate infant bath tub inside a 'big people' one. Make sure that our bathing areas are very clean and sanitary and do an extra rinse for the residue, especially if foods have been prepared in the kitchen sink. This is most important if there was raw meat and/or eggs in the sink.

We are still neither able to sit up yet, nor hold our heads up without support. Please, NEVER leave us alone in a tub of water of any kind. We can drown in ONE-HALF INCH OF WATER OR LESS! Never leave us unattended! Since we are in water now instead of a dry bath, please use our baby bath thermometers to be sure that the water is not too hot for our skin. Make sure that we are still bathed with infant shampoos and baby washes, like 'Johnson & Johnson'™ soft wash baby wash or Dove™ baby wash.

Both of these washes have lotion in them, so if we live in a drier climate, this could be helpful in keeping our baby skin moist. Infant bath products should be made to have a pH balance equivalent to that of water, meaning that it should not burn our eyes.

Continuing on with skin, it must be understood that our skin is fresh and new. Our skin has not been weathered like that of the mommies and daddies around us. We must have sun block on us whenever we go outside, especially in the sun. We can get burned within 15 minutes of sun exposure, even in overcast weather. This includes just an afternoon walk in our stroller. Umbrella strollers have canopies that help protect us from the sun. Hats and sunglasses do a great job, too, as long as we keep them on. We can't make any promises on that one.

Here's another hint - if the sun is out, and there is either snow, water, or a light sandy beach, try to get sunglasses for us to wear because our eyes can get sunburned! Not just yours, ours too! This does not happen nearly as often as getting a sunburn on the skin, but it can happen. Just remember we are much more sensitive to everything than you are!

Hopefully, we are putting on good baby fat. We may

also have extra 'rolls' in our thighs, neck, arms, and knees. These areas are more sensitive to skin irritation. This is recognized by redness appearing in these areas and sometimes, they become raw. If this happens late at night, and the doctor is not available, you can help relieve this irritation by putting some medicated diaper powder on these areas, after a cooling bath. If there are some raw areas, use a light bit of diaper rash ointment before putting some powder on top. These areas should clear relatively quickly, following these special 'hints' and keeping us out of 'hot weather'. Overly bundled attire, which creates sweat prolonging the irritation. If the condition persists, make a list of questions to ask the doctor or nurse practitioner.

It is possible to begin some 'tummy time' now. This is time that we spend on our bellies to give us more strength in our stomach, back, arms and neck. We will begin to be able to hold our heads up on our own for a few seconds. This is very good. For tummy time, place us on a comfortable blanket or in a play pen and do not have it be longer than a few minutes because it is very tiring. Hint, we don't recommend doing this right after we eat because we will most likely spit up right away. Messy scenario!

Huge Hint! This is the time when we start going on our

first outings outside of doctor visits. Let us tell you, there has been a huge survey of all babies over the last few years to determine the best, top-of-the-line feeding and nursing facility available at shopping malls. There was a landslide winner, that we believe can take home the prize. We are so excited to announce the winner is ....NORDSTROM™! That's right, Nordstrom™. It is an upscale department store located in many malls all over the United States. They were thinking of us (you and me) when they laid out the plans for their restrooms. There are usually family restrooms, but the ladies' restroom is the best! Their ladies' restrooms have an additional room off to the side, after you walk in, for mothers with babies.

Mothers can go in there and pump, if you want to, in a relaxing atmosphere while sitting on a couch. You can also breast or bottle feed us, change our diaper, and relax with us in cozy environment away from the hustle and bustle of the mall shopping experience. This is a perfect location for us to have some down time. We would like to thank Nordstrom™, their president, managers, and architects for such a wonderful job. Kudos to you!!!

Chapter 5

Month Three

Here we are sliding in to the end of our first trimester! Oops, that already happened. We mean our first trimester with you! That's it! Boy, we are coming right along and you are doing a great job, too! Remember to give us hugs and kisses everyday and tell us how much you love us because we would not be able to grow as well without all of that from you! Thank you, thank you, thank you! We are continuing on a regular diet of breast milk and/or formula feedings. Now, we may have a reaction to our formulas. Please speak with our pediatrician if we are constantly vomiting or having diarrhea after our feedings. This is a tell-tale sign we may be having an allergic reaction to our formula. For our breast-feeding mothers, you still need to be careful of eating the gaseous foods, very spicy foods and large amounts of caffeine (coffee, soda, caffeinated tea). The caffeine over-stimulates us, the vegetables give us gas, and the spicy delicacies which upsets our bellies. Either way, it is not a good outcome once it goes through us.

Here is another important piece of information! If you have two or more drinks, whether it is beer, wine, shots of liquor, or mixed drinks, do not breast-feed us! Pump the breast milk and pour it down the sink for twenty-four hours after consuming this amount of alcohol before going back to regular feedings. During this time, supplement us with formula. Please, make sure that there is a sober adult available to care for us.

Sometimes, you may not know you are going to be having an upset stomach. There are instances where we will start to have an upset belly, then you will start to have an upset belly about an hour later. Funny thing, isn't it? Our digestive track is much smaller than yours, so we will have the symptoms first. Unfortunately for us, it is like we are your warning sign of eating discomforting foods.

Do not be concerned if we do not have daily bowel movements, that is okay. We may not have a bowel movement for four or more days, especially if we are breast-fed. This is not something that happens with all of us, it does happen. However, if you are concerned, please call our pediatrician. We do not recommend, AT ALL, that you purchase some over-the-counter suppositories and use them without calling the doctor. Again, this can be dangerous to our very small digestive system.

But, let's move on to some great things about our third month. We may be starting to sleep for some longer periods of time. We may sleep for six hours during the night before waking for a feeding. Wahoo! We may also take a longer nap during the day and be up for longer periods than we have been. This means you are able to have a more restful sleep, too.

No matter if we are a boy or a girl, please tell us how beautiful we are every day. Tell us how much you love us, too! That is the best thing to say to us every day, even if you were very busy and we did not get to see each other much. We know you are talking to us and every time you say these beautiful words to us, we are being wrapped in your love. Even in these newest precious days, this give us confidence, self-esteem and the ability to grow into wonderful big people like yourselves! You, our moms, dads, grandparents, aunts, uncles, siblings and the like, shape and mold who we are now, who we will become, and the path we will take to get there. Remember to shower us with love every day, even when we are eighteen years old. This builds communication and conversation between us. Communication, trust and openness between us will be the ground work on which we will grow together.

The very special part of this, right now, is we will start to respond to you. We are able to see you more clearly and in color. We trust you very much. You are our life. We try to let you know by cooing and smiling at you. We hear you and love you, too.

We understand having our life in your hands is a huge responsibility, but we love you and we trust you will love us, too. You will be rewarded with watching what you create through us.

This is also a perfect time to learn to say the word 'sorry'. We learn compassion, forgiveness and responsibility for our actions, especially if they affect others in a harmful way. If you get upset with us and raise your voice , we cry louder because we feel change in your pitch and emotion. Please go and take ten minutes for yourself, after putting us in a 'safe place'. When you come back, say you are sorry, and tell us you love us. This is for both of us to learn how to show love through an apology. Nobody is perfect 100% of the time and it is okay as long as you can say 'sorry'. Thank you so much for learning this. We love you.

For a change of pace, nursery rhymes like 'Patty-Cake' and 'Rock-a-Bye-Baby' are great to introduce. We smile and coo along with you. We will watch how your mouth moves and how your eyes dance while you sing to us. If you have to put off doing the dishes to spend a few minutes singing with us, great. We won't complain! As you are singing these songs to us, we are also learning the words, the tempo of the song and the dancing body movements. It is so cute to watch us learn how to clap along with you. One day soon, we will be trying to repeat these songs back to you!

Tummy time is very important right now. This is where we lay down on the floor for a few minutes each day. We will probably get mad, but we are strengthening our neck muscles. We are also stretching back, arm and leg muscles. Afterwards, if you have time, roll us to our backside and give us a nice lotion massage to help relax our muscles and calm us at the same time. It would be wonderful if you would join us down here, too!

This is also a good time to introduce a 'kick-start gym' to us. Kick-start gyms have toys that we can kick with our feet to start songs and/or watch lights begin to dance. We love watching the different colors appear and songs play because of our own movements! We may not understand the whole concept, however, this is our beginning.

Many kick-start gyms have mobile-like toys that hang down from an arc-shaped bar, usually used by you to carry the gym. When you turn us around to where our heads lay (where our feet were just kicking), the bar with the mobile toys should be hanging just over our heads. To us, it looks as though these toys are close enough for us to touch, so we try stretching and reaching to grasp the toys. When we make it to the toy and it spins, we did it! It is so cool! Look what else we can do! Who knew how many senses and motor skills we would be using! Each one of these exercises, and good play time, increases our brain and muscle development every day.

Just to explain a little more in-depth about ourselves, 'gross motor skills' are the development of our larger muscles. These would include our legs, stomach, neck, back and arm muscles. 'Fine motor skills' are the development of our fingers and toes, the smaller muscles that we use. When developing fine motor skills, you are looking for pinching and grasping abilities. Such examples would include being able to scoop, or pick up, a block or a piece of toasted oat cereal.

'Intellectual development' is our brain area of development where we process 'problem-solving' techniques. Problem-solving has many different areas of development, including how to roll over to reach a toy, what button to push to start up the lights on a toy, and figuring out where our toy went after it was removed from our line-of-sight. As we keep growing in our first year, you will see new levels of development in all of these areas.

Last but not least, is our 'social and emotional development'. Our social development includes talking to you, whoever chooses to visit, and whether we are affected by our visitors. Our emotional development includes how we feel about the situation we are in at any given time. This includes, how we act if you leave the room or how long we may cry if we are upset and you are trying to comfort us. Our 'temperament' falls into this category. To describe 'temperament', this includes how quickly we will get upset and how long we stay upset. If we can be distracted while we are upset and how quickly we calm down after being upset. Generally, a good clue in this area is that most of us can be distracted while we are upset.

This can be done by walking outside, singing or jingling car keys near us, usually we will get distracted. If we cannot be distracted, something is definitely upsetting us. Check for a diaper rash, if we are hungry, or a fever and if we are pulling on our ear, we may have an ear infection and you should call the doctor right away. Normally though, it is something simple that a little distraction, followed up with some special attention, can easily cure.

We are trying to make sure that we are giving you all the information we can at the appropriate times where the information would be used best. However, we all develop differently so we are doing the best we can. We do want to mention something to look out for, that truly can happen at anytime, and until we are much older. Sometimes, when we are about to get a cold or an ear infection, you will see ear wax build up from the outside of our ear. At these times, use a cotton swab and clean just the outside of the ear that you can see. You do not want to stick the cotton swab inside our ear because you can cause inner-ear damage and that would be horrible. This is kind of a funny trick, but if you catch this on the day that it shows, often it goes away by the next day (so do some other symptoms. Like we said, this information can last for years. Cool, huh?).

We do feel that we have just given you a considerable amount of information for this month, but as the old saying goes, ‘knowledge is power’. The more hints and information we give you will hopefully create the confidence you need to know you are doing great. We relish in the comfort of your strength. Good job, everyone!

Chapter 6

Month Four

This is the month for new experiences, ugly faces, lots of spitting up and thicker stools. Oh, and you are wondering what makes this month different? We can be introduced to cereal. Not the cereal that is for, well, bigger people than us, but baby cereal. As long as we have gotten the 'okay' from our doctor, then let's start with the introductions!

Baby cereal is very, very flaky. It is generally sold only in the baby food aisle, not in the adult and child cereal aisle. To reiterate, baby cereal is not, nor will ever be, fruit-flavored rings, apple rings, cinnamon crunch squares, and all of the many other cereals of this type. We hope you get the point that it is not like 'table food'. When trying to introduce our baby cereal to us, it is a very messy thing, so be prepared with a bib for us, and maybe you, as well.

Let's get serious about this. There are rice cereals, oatmeal, mixed cereals and general baby cereals. Always for infants! Now, there are some guidelines you need to follow. The American Pediatrics Association recommends that we weigh at least 13 pounds before we are introduced to cereal. It is also highly recommended that we are able to hold our head up with our own neck strength before attempting to feed us cereal. These guidelines help to keep us from being sick, be able to swallow, and to be able to move our head to let you know when we have had enough. These are just guidelines; although they are very important, they may not be absolutes.

If you are still breast-feeding us, do not stop. Breast-feed us for the whole year, if you are able to. The rewards are tremendous! Do not feed us cereal to replace our formula/breast milk feedings. This will be too much for us to digest. We can gain weight too fast and possibly have problems digesting.

Cereal is to be mixed in a bowl with a spoon with either breast milk or formula. Breast milk will have to be pumped in order to be mixed with cereal and note that breast milk is a little watery. Only introduce cereal for one feeding first, like dinner, followed with breast milk or formula. It is best to have cereal fed to us with a spoon, so that we can learn how to swallow from eating off of a spoon. The swallowing reflex is a different reflex than sucking on a nipple, which becomes activated when we are trying to swallow something that has substance. This is very different than swallowing just liquid. This is easily explained as learning to move our tongue around in our mouth, with the food, to our throat. Please, make sure that you are using a 'baby size' spoon. A larger size will not fit in our mouth and could be a choking hazard because a larger spoon will hold more cereal than we may be able to swallow.

If you are breast-feeding and you are not ready to work cereal into our routine yet, that is okay by us. We are still getting all of your nutrients and antibodies. Did you know, way back in the day (and many cultures still do), we were breast-fed for a few years? It helps many of us to stay healthy by getting the nourishment we need.

So, let's go over the essentials: baby cereal is BABY cereal (not any other type of cereal), it's best that we are at a good weight of 13 pounds; we have good control of our heads; we have doctor's approval; and we are fed in an Upright Position! It is perfectly okay to place us in a swing or our bouncer chair to set us into an upright position. Do not replace all of our feedings with cereal. It is mandatory to keep up with our formula/breast-feedings. Now do you think you have all the information you need? Great! We are so excited! You are doing a wonderful job!

Some of our parents are deciding whether are not to go back to work. Let us just say there is nothing greater than to have one of you at home for the first five years of our lives. We get everything from you. Our self-esteem, confidence, love, communication, support and nurturing are priceless commodities that carry us through the rest of our lives. If you can make it happen, please, please, do. You will never regret it. All of our 'first times' only happen once and we want to share them all with you. You are our first teachers in life; our confidence and our trust begins with you.

If you are unable to stay at home for whatever reason, please make sure that we are taken to a safe place. If you have an uncomfortable feeling about a place where you are taking us, even though it was recommended to you by someone you trust, don't take us in there! Please, check these places out! Do interviews before you hand us over to caretakers. You are handing our lives over to them; take the time to get to know them. We can't say enough to trust your instincts (yes, this would be the 'parent' voice inside of you).

They are your best guides in these types of situations.

Make sure if we are taken to a day care center, the facility is a place that has been certified by the state as a licensed day care provider. Also, be certain that someone is on hand who is certified in baby/infant CPR and first aid. This includes relatives, good friends, grandmas and grandpas. We are very tiny, our first aid and emergency needs are much different than yours. The repetitions of CPR for an adult is exactly same the amount that is required for one of us. But, *how* the breaths are given are different for one of us than for an adult. Hand and finger placement for the compressions are <u>very different.</u> If the hand placement for the compressions are performed on us in the same manner as an adult, IT WILL CRUSH OUR RIB CAGE!! This is why we address this matter so strongly! The difference is, literally, lifesaving! If the caregiver does not know the difference in how to give breaths, do not leave us in their care!

Most hospitals hold classes on baby/infant CPR and first aid. You can take the class with the caregiver and your spouse so you all will have the knowledge. We highly recommend learning these skills as it is always better to be prepared. There are situations where time is of the essence.

These classes can save our lives. Remember, we still cannot tell you when something is wrong. Our lives are in your hands. If you follow these simple hints, we truly believe that you will be able to find a great person to take care of us while you are at work.

Let's see, what else happens in month four? Oh, yeah, more great stuff! It is important that if you lay us down we are not put somewhere where we could fall off! That's right because we are absolutely trying to roll over. Typically, the first roll-overs start from tummy to back, then back to tummy. You can help by dangling a toy over our head then slowly bringing it over to the side for us to follow and hopefully, roll-over. It doesn't matter which way to roll that we learn first, just as long as we are learning it! You can help us out with this during our tummy times, too. Our tummy times should not be such a horrible experience now. We should be getting used to it. (Note - we still wouldn't recommend this play time to be held after we eat or we will still spit up on the floor). Having playtime, either on a floor or in a playpen, is so beneficial for strengthening, stretching, and developing our muscles. After our tummy times, gym play or a bath, it is still good to give us a little massage with baby lotion.

Massaging us is a wonderful thing to do. Besides

relaxing our muscles after we are trying to use them, massage can relax us when we are just upset. Sometimes, when we have a belly-ache gently stroke your fingertips over and around our bellies can be very comforting. If you have the opportunity, take a 'baby massage' class or have a session with a licensed massage therapist. They can teach you neat methods of massaging us that can be healing and soothing. The special benefits of this, is the time we will spend together with the amazing power of your touch. Thank you for all of the wonderful things you are doing for us!

Hey, have you noticed that we are bouncing, bouncing, bouncing everywhere we can? If you are holding us up on our feet, we are bouncing! A 'Johnny Jumper' or some kind of jumping gym might be just the kick we need!

Now, we are trying to sit up a little, like when we are sitting in your lap and we get to do sing-alongs with you. We get sit in your lap and use our hands, and yours, to do nursery rhymes and clap! We love clapping and happy times! Clap often and make up funny songs, we love it! Making up songs are great because you made them just for us! Now that we can see you so much better we love to hear your voice, especially in song. We cannot express to you enough just how great this is!

Here is something new to introduce to you. Have us sit in your lap in front of a mirror. (We will grow to LOVE mirrors!) We will reach out to the mirror to try to touch our face and yours. Being able to see what happens in front of a mirror is simply amazing to us. Point to us, show us our face, head, nose, mouth and cheeks. Name each body part as you are pointing them out and do the same thing with yourself. Point to your eyes, nose, mouth and hair. Mix it up a little bit and constantly take us back to the mirror and name off our body parts. As we keep getting older, we will learn and recognize them.

Point to yourself and say your name, then point to us and say ours. Feel free to ad-lib by saying 'beautiful', 'handsome' or 'pretty baby'. We will learn to love those names, too. Using mirrors is a great learning tool for us. (This a big hint coming, so take notes if you need to.) We can discover and explore through mirrors. We will adore what we look like, just as you love what we look like, too. Telling us how beautiful we are in a mirror will stay with us through our lives and will start us on the right path of self-acceptance. If we ever have a bad day, put us in front of the mirror and remind us we are beautiful. Just so you know, we believe you are the most beautiful men and women in the world, even on your worst day. You are the kings and queens of our world. The greatest part of our knowledge of 'beauty' is that we already know it is not just skin deep.

Chapter 7

Month Five

Stretch those legs and kick, kick, kick! Now reach, reach, reach! Oh, hey there! We were just doing our exercises. Would you like to join us? It's pretty fun actually. We love people who get on the floor and join us. Everybody says there is not enough time to exercise. Well, here is a little hint to figure that out. Some moms and dads go to gyms, not the kick-gyms we use, but big people gyms in order to get their exercise. However, you can get some exercise right here with us! That's right, *with* us! Some people have excercise videos to do at home. We personally recommend something like pilates or yoga, where you spend a lot of time on the floor. Just like we do! We have our blanket and you have yours, or mats, or whatever. The way this works is we get to do it together!

Some of you wait until we are napping to do your exercises. We need to tell you that this really works well together. We will laugh, giggle and roll around with you. We will kick our feet and try to roll back and forth - it's a blast! Together, we strengthen our stomach, back, leg and arm muscles. This gets us ready to sit up independently and to start crawling, for that is coming really soon. Put aside time for this everyday, if you can, or at least a few times a week. See, you get your exercise and we get to have fun with you on the floor working on our muscles. Your exercise, and our tummy time, become one of our rituals! Boy, how many greater things can you put together?

Just a note, if you, or both of us, are having a bad day, exercise! Exercise is a great stress reliever and it sends off endorphins from your brain to your body. Endorphins are what the body creates to naturally better your mood. Plus, you release a lot of stress by working it out of your body. Here is a great idea for ANYTIME! Put on a great song and get to shaking your booty! Laugh, dance and smile. Now, doesn't that feel good? You bet it does!

Instead of exercising while we are napping, you now have time to return, or make important phone calls, write letters, or respond to e-mails while we are resting.

We are paying attention to sounds a little better now. Music can be a really cool way for us to understand rhythm. Try all kinds of music; classical, jazz, hip-hop, top 40, big band, anything! If it has a beat, then we can bounce to it! We can also try to clap or swing our arms to the rhythm of the beat. We also enjoy homemade music, such as the songs that you sing to us, jingling of keys, cool rattles, chimes, bells, drums, pots and pans! Please remember you should not play anything too loud because we can still get frightened and startled by loud noises. Also, music and noise are good distractions from a bad mood, especially when you enjoy the music with us.

Moving to our 'skills section', place our toys a little out of our reach so that we try to get them. You can lay about three of them in sequential order where one is a little further away from the other. Once we try to reach one and get it, then we will reach for the other one behind it. Our gross motor skills are getting stronger every day and by doing each of these little playtimes, we are also improving on our fine motor skills. To touch base on that again, our gross motor skills are our larger muscles: stomach, back, legs and arms and fine motor skills - small muscles: hands, fingers and toes. Our 'grasping' abilities stemming from our fine motor skills are becoming much better. We can hold our bottles and rattles. You can also give us a double-handled beginner sip cup to try our holding abilities.

With our foods and nutrition, abide by our pediatrician's recommendations per our check-ups or well visits. Since we are in our fifth month, most of us have tried to eat cereal and have been able to swallow while being fed from a spoon. By this time, unless there is a particular reason given to you by our doctor, you can start to add some juice to our bottle or to our cereal with breast milk/formula. To us, it would taste like strawberry cream oatmeal or something like that. Here is a guideline - our juice should be nothing but 100% JUICE! Juice is NOT drink mix, lemonade, tea or any juice with 10% juice.

It is best that our juice be mixed with half water when it is introduced to us in our bottles. There are a few benefits to doing it this way; for example, the juice lasts longer. At the beginning, the juice may be a little too acidic for our bellies (meaning it could upset our stomachs). If it is hot outside, or we are feeling a bit warm, we will be getting some vitamins mixed with water making sure we are maintaining our hydration. (Hydration has to do with how much water our bodies have inside. When we run a fever, have diarrhea, or are sweating a lot, our bodies are losing our internal water/moisture. These conditions dry us from the inside out and it is very important that we re-hydrate to get it back.)

For us babies, one way to know if we are starting to become dehydrated, other than the above mentioned reasons, is that our urine will have a much stronger odor to it. You will notice this! Please contact our doctor if our fever, or diarrhea, is not going away. We may need other types of hydration, such as an IV. An 'IV' stands for Intravenous Fluids, given to us in a hospital through a needle, if we become severely dehydrated. The good thing is that our bodies absorb this quickly to help get us back to normal. Therefore, it is always wise to make sure we are hydrated at all times.

Ask our pediatrician for tips on how to check if we are hydrated, such as pushing on our fingertip fat to see that it bounces back out. Our doctor can help you learn about the different levels of hydration and how to notice them, especially if we live in very hot or dry climates. This doesn't mean that we need to have something in our mouth every second of the day, but pay attention to these unique scenarios. This is another reason why we explain the importance of paying attention to the temperature outside.

Back to continuing information, if we are still being breast-fed, continue to do this! Formula, too! Do not change us over to just juice, water and cereal. Our bodies very much still need the nourishment that comes from breast milk and formula. Everything else is only an addition to these core necessities. At about the age of twelve months, we can start to have whole milk to replace formula and breast-feedings. (Replacing the breast-feedings is a choice, however, whole milk could also be included with a meal and 'worked' in). Of course, this is under our pediatrician's guidance.

Just a note, if we are experiencing a bad cough, try to give us less breast milk/formula and more juice and water combinations. Milk and milky liquids cause more build up in the back of our throats, especially from a cough *and* a runny/stuffy nose. This makes it a little more difficult to be able to clear up our cough, and nasal and swallowing areas when milk is mixed with a build up of mucus. This is very important information!

Purchase only ONE flavor of bottled juice at a time. By flavor, we mean berry, apple, or grape juice. It is possible that we can have a different reaction to every type of juice, just like everything else. You should see any reaction that we may have within twenty-four hours of consumption. Normally, our reaction will come in the form of a diaper or some version of a skin rash. If we break out in a diaper rash, do not continue to give us that flavor of juice. As mentioned previously, we recommend that our juice is mixed half with water. The other good thing about this is if we do have a diaper rash from our juice, the rash will be less severe if the juice has been mixed with water before we consumed it. This is a good tip!

Quickly touching base on dealing with diaper rashes; if our rash is *severe* (severe meaning there are raw areas), put baby powder on first. The talc in the powder will absorb the moisture in our raw areas. *(Did you know that the original barber-surgeons used talcum powder to stop bleeding on open wounds? Feel comforted that it will help us, too.)* After applying the powder, put on the diaper rash ointment if it is necessary. Be wary of putting us in a bath with very warm water if we have raw spots. We believe it is better if the water is on the cooler side so it does not burn our sensitive area(s). If we get a rash that is really bad, please, feel free to take us to our doctor where they may prescribe a diaper rash ointment.

So, how are you doing? Any questions? You are very

lucky if everything is perfect every day but, in the real world, you may need to ask our grandparents, or uncles, or friends to help out. Believe the old saying, it does take a village to raise us! Do not be discouraged at any time with us or yourself; we love you so much! We know you will figure it out and we hope we are giving you some great tools to use! Bravo!

Chapter 8

Six Months Old!

Six months old, six months old, we are six months old! Who loves us? You do! And who do we love? You! What a great cheer to do with us each morning. How are you doing? Are you sleeping a little better at night? That's great! If not, then start to lay us down in our crib at the same time each night after we have had our dinner, burp, bath, book, songs or whatever our nighttime schedule consists of.

Mainly, we are doing this to stop the one middle of the night feeding, so we can sleep longer through the night. As stated before, do not put us in our crib with a bottle. It is harmful to our teeth, our ability to breathe, can cause us to choke and is a contributing factor to ear infections. We will probably wake up at the time we normally feed and we will cry, do not be surprised. It is always a longer cry on the first night than any other (possibly for you, too). If we cry longer than twenty minutes, it is okay to come in and check on us to make sure we do not have a wet diaper, fever or are chilly. You do not have to take us out of the crib to check on us. To reiterate, the first night is the roughest when you are ready to have us stay in our own room. However, this is a guide, not an absolute as to when we should be in our own bed all night. We are all just as individual as all of you. Even at this age, some of us still eat three times during the night, or may be going through a growth spurt and insist on nighttime nourishment. Keep in mind what is most important, that we are getting the sleep we need, which is between 14-15 hours each day.

Wow, we are six months old! Sorry we keep shouting it out, but what a profound age for us! We are trying to jump when you hold us under our armpits, if we haven't been doing this for weeks already. We can roll over from back to front and front to back. We are pulling our legs up underneath us and rocking back and forth. Some of us are doing an 'army-crawl' (while we are on our stomach, we use one or both arms to pull us across the floor while pushing with our legs). We should be sitting up pretty well on our own and this is so good, especially for mirror, clapping, and singing time. If we are sitting up without your assistance, please place pillows around us in case we topple over, thank you. We are also cooing, clapping, singing, smiling and enjoying being six months old. We just love it as much as you do. Isn't this so much fun?!

You say our name and we turn our heads to see you. We are drooling, teething, biting and picking up small objects. Small objects are the ones you need to be careful about. From this point on, make sure not to have anything around us that we can reach, put in our mouth and swallow. At the store you can purchase a 'small objects' tester. These testers are normally in the shape of a round tube or cylinder. You put small objects inside the tube, and if it fits in, then it is too small for us and is a choking hazard. Keep these items out of our reach. We can pick up toasted oat cereal or small baby puff snacks and we can eat these items, too!

We love to play games like peek-a-boo because we are trying to do them *with* you now. You see, being able to share experiences with you is one of the most wonderful things about being six months old. Interacting with you is always a growing point. Now that we have better control of our heads, we can sit in our high chairs at the table to enjoy our meals with you. We are eating our own meals though, not yours, but we are eating with you just the same. Since we are on the subject, let's talk about new foods.

That's right, we said new foods! On the okay from our pediatrician to start our 'new foods', let's take a trip to the grocery store. At the grocery store, look for 'stage 1' foods or 'first stage'. These jars of baby foods are made with one food item in their ingredients, such as bananas, pears, apples, or green beans. Not mixed together. It is best to pick a color of foods to start with, such as jars of food that are green in color, or orange, or yellow. You must start with only one food first, testing it for about 3 or 4 days. This is to see if we have a reaction to it, in the same manner that everything else is introduced. A full blown allergic reaction is not a prominent response, but an upset stomach or diaper rash is more likely. This is why it is so important to introduce the foods on an individual basis and give each food a few days on its own before having us try a new one. Do not season our food either; this includes salt, pepper and sugar. Our baby food is specifically made to not have any 'additional' ingredients. As we are so pure, so should the foods and drinks we take in.

Some mommies and daddies may want to make their own baby food. Terrific! Here are some hints on how to make our foods so we may digest them. If you are making vegetables, steam them first. This way, you keep all of the natural vitamins and nutrients. It is recommended not to start with potatoes or tomatos. If you need a hint on what foods to start with, take a trip to the grocery store and see what foods they have listed in their 'first stage' jars and take it from there.

After the foods are prepared by steaming, puree' them in a blender with a little water. To be honest, getting the perfect consistency may take a few tries, so start with adding a little bit of water at a time until you get there. You will also need to get some baby jars, or very small plastic containers, to put the food in. Some stores do have baby food pureers that clamp onto the top of a baby jar and you churn the food from there. This way, the food is already in the jar. If you prepare your own baby food, do not just place it in a cupboard without an airtight jar sealer, but instead place it in the refrigerator. We wouldn't recommend making more than a couple of days' worth of baby food at a time.

Please note not all foods need to be steamed, just pureed. (Mainly fruits fall into this category). Preparing foods at home, once you have the mixture down. It is pretty easy to do with apples, bananas, green beans, squash, sweet potatoes, peaches, and carrots (plus others). That is a good start. If you are nervous about preparing the food, there are many cookbooks for making infant food or there may be a book that our pediatrician recommends. To sum up, if you are looking to prepare our foods yourself, there are plenty of resources out there to help you.

One of the first ways to tell if we are having an allergic reaction to anything we may eat or drink is to look at our skin first. (This is a lifelong lesson.) Our skin will react with a rash, sometimes just in our diaper, or it can show up anywhere. The rashes may be in one particular area or spread all over the body. These rashes will hang around for about a day. They usually consist of tiny red bumps or the skin just appears red in color. We may also get hives.

Hives can be large in size. The unique difference between hives and a rash are hives will move around the body. This is one of its tell-tale signs. For instance, you could be changing our diaper and notice red bumps, or patches, all over our belly. Two hours later during our next changing, it seems the bumps have left our stomach. Do not be frightened if you turn us over to find the bumps on our back and legs. Again, hives are usually gone in 24 hours, like a rash, without any form of treatment.

Similar to a rash, it is hard to diagnose exactly what causes hives based on their origination. Hives can surface internally on rare occasions. Watch for swelling in the mouth. If you see this, take us straight to the doctor. This can clog our airways! This is rare, but keep this information in the back of your mind. It is much easier to tell what gives us hives if we are introduced to foods one at a time, every few days. Typically, many of us don't have any allergic reaction to foods or juices. However, if we have red bumps and a fever at the same time, this would be the time to call our pediatrician.

We still need our breast milk/formula feedings. We are very thirsty little babies! We are very much in need of our main source of vitamins and nutrients. We are still requiring eight breast milk/formula feedings per day.

Here at the six months mark, we are developing our fine motor skills further. This is a really good time for us to be trying out neat shape sorters. We can figure out moving the shapes around and then placing them in the right spots. When you are playing these games with us, it is never too early to tell us the shapes and colors of the toys we have. There are also blocks and balls that have multiple colors on the outside and neat things on the inside, such as tiny trucks, jingle balls, sand and dice. This is so cool! We get to shake, rattle, and roll with our toys.

Another neat thing to introduce to us are wood puzzles. Get the wood puzzles that have really bright colors and each piece has its own individual knob attached to help us be able to hold it. These puzzles have specific spots for each piece to be put in, with your help, we learn to twirl and twist the piece until it fits perfectly into the puzzle. Make sure that the pieces of the puzzle are not just covered in paper because we will probably chew them off after we cover the paper in slobber. Now this is important, having you play with us to show us how to do it. Otherwise we can get frustrated because we do not know how to play with it. Thank you kindly for your guidance!

Do not worry if we are not doing movements or grasping at the exact times as described in this book. The motor skills and social/emotional developments are guidelines to help let you know where we should be, but allow a two month window. Normal development for a six-month-old can start anywhere between five and seven months. At our check-ups, our pediatrician will ask you simple questions like if we have rolled over yet. Keep our pediatrician updated with our movements and developments and let them know at any time any concerns you might have. That is why it is very important to have floor play with us, to clap and sing with us, and to notice if we are responding to you and the world around us.

Chapter 9

Seventh Month

Listen closely.... did you hear that? It sounded like "Da-da". Did you hear "Ma-ma"? We thought we heard it, too. We have been trying to tell you these words. We are hoping that our words will become more clear this month. While you are sitting with us, make simple sounds, or repetitive ones, like 'da-da-da'. We are following your mouth movement and sound. We are trying to repeat back to you what we see and hear.

If you feel you still haven't had time to bond with us, then do it now. This is so important. If you have not taken the time to do the many things with us that we have addressed in this book, the time is now! For seven months, we have been trying to contact you through any and all means we have available to us. Our life, love, and support system comes from you. Let's have a baby weekend. Just for us to really get to know each other, without the interruption of everyday life. We know nothing about this part of life. Our life is you.

Follow us around with a camera and take lots of pictures. If you have some sort of video camera, film us for about twenty minutes, preferably awake for this lesson. You can see life differently through the lens of a camera. In daily life, you know that we are rolling, rocking, tumbling and sitting. Through a lens, sometimes you can watch just how we think. It's amazing! (This is a clue.) While you are recording, put items around us to reach for and play with or sing a nursery rhyme, and watch what we do. Funny, it is like taking yourself out of the picture and seeing the world through our eyes. After video taping, watch it again with us. Watch how we react to ourselves and you get to watch us, too! This is a wonderful way to experience our life with us.

Hey, do you see what we are doing now? We believe this is called crawling, or for some, 'scooting' would be the term to use. Some of us are sitting up really well and instead of falling over, we are intentionally going over to our side to be on our hands and knees. Isn't that so cool? Don't forget our bouncing, bouncing, bouncing! It almost makes you dizzy if you watch long enough.

How are we doing with our 'new foods'? We should have gotten through one food color by this time and are ready to start another. Of course, this is based on the okay from our pediatrician. We are still having breast milk/formula feedings and also our 'pick-up' snacks.

A few of us may have our first tooth, but if not, look for it to possibly show up this month and into the next. Here's a hint, keep a wet washcloth inside a sandwich bag in the refrigerator so we can have something to gnaw on when the pain is unbearable. Some parents hold a juice popsicle for us to cool our gums on while other parents put our pacifier in the refrigerator. If we are having an especially hard time going to sleep or are just uncomfortable with the whole teething thing, there are gum-numbing ointments. You can use infant ibuprofen (especially if a fever is our reaction to the teething), or an oral infant pain reliever to help with our discomfort. Please help us by rubbing our gums if you can see the white of our teeth trying to come through. Our teeth can try to come up and break through the gum a number of times before finally breaking the surface and appearing. Once the initial teeth break through, the rest generally come through with more ease, except the molars may give us some difficulty. Generally speaking though, our front teeth come in first, whether it's top or bottom; again, this is a guideline to go by. Some of us will not get our first tooth until we are twelve months old, others at six months. Either way, our teeth are coming!

Once we get our first tooth and you are breast-feeding us, do we bite? To be honest, it does happen. Please, do not be so fearful that you stop breast-feeding us, we do not even have a mouthful of teeth yet. If we do bite down while feeding, place your finger inside our mouth to pry it open or gently tickle us if there is a tickle spot you know of, we will open our mouth. DO NOT SHAKE, THROW OR SMACK US! We do not know what it means to have these things called teeth. We could not possibly understand what it means now when we 'gum down'.

You can tell us "Ow!", if we happen to bite. Oddly enough, we will get it, though maybe not the first or second time, but we will. Generally, most of us do not bite every time we nurse. In fact, it is more of a rarity than a normal occurrence. If you are still breast-feeding us, do not stop just because we have teeth. We will lose all the vitamins and antibodies we receive from your breastmilk. Like we said, we will learn the word 'Ow' and it won't be a problem anymore.

Breast-milk and formula are still our main sources of daily nutrition.

Since we are becoming more mobile and some of us may be starting to pull ourselves up, let's pay attention to what is around us. Please know you need to watch out for corners on tables, especially coffee and end tables. There are furniture 'corner covers' you can purchase to put on the corners of these tables. The covers are made from a clear rubber that takes the 'point' off. We recommend getting the covers if you have these kinds of tables. The other thing to remember is we are still easily distracted. If we are heading towards or are in a dangerous area, you could shake a rattle ten feet away to distract us and guide us in a different direction.

Speaking of danger - Very Important Information - NEVER place us near a fireplace with a lit fire or leave us alone near one! We do not understand that fire is hot, but we understand bright dancing light. We can be burned severely, possibly putting us in the hospital. Do not give us paper or any items that can catch on fire, if we are near one. (Big hint: If we are ever burned, run the area under cool water. If a blister emerges, that is a second degree burn and we need medical treatment immediately. DO NOT POP THE

BLISTER AT ALL, NO MATTER HOW BIG IT IS! Third degree burns can appear white, black or 'singed-looking' and needs immediate medical attention. Call our doctor or go straight to an emergency medical facility if we ever suffer a second or third degree burn.)

Now following up after the fire information, we will talk about our clothing for a minute. Most infants' clothing is made from flame-retardant material, but some clothing items are not. Please read the tag. We can only ask that you just DO NOT purchase these clothes and we will not have to worry as much about our clothing catching fire from being near a match or candle. This is very dangerous! Also, make sure you pay attention to what you are wearing if you are holding us and are near any source of fire. We would feel terrible if we did not address this matter and it occurred. We would much rather be safe and INFORMED than in danger and ignorant.

That should have cleared up another important topic. And so, how are you doing? Are you feeling okay? We hope so. We do understand having even ONE of us can be extremely overwhelming. It's perfectly reasonable and healthy to get a trustworthy baby-sitter and take a night out on the town or treat yourself to a spa. (Funny how many times you think of us while you are gone. We love you, too.)

When it comes to being sick, you will be able to see some ways to check if you need to take us to our doctor. Our doctor should be pretty thorough to make sure we do not receive antibiotics for a simple cold. Simple colds need to run their course in order for us to further build our immunities. It has been shown that if we take too many antibiotics now through four to seven years old, those antibiotics will not be *nearly* as effective to us as young adults and adults. Our bodies will develop an immunity to antibiotics because we have taken so many while we were young. They become part of our natural defense system. Our bodies need to fight off smaller common viruses, like colds, to build up immunities. This helps to insure the antibiotics will be effective when we become sick with something we really need antibiotics for.

A runny nose should be taken care of at home. For stuffy or runny noses that last longer than five days, call our doctor and see if they wish to see us. Runny noses that have clear mucus are not a big concern. This can happen just from being sweaty. If the mucus is green or greenish-yellow coming out of our nose, this means we are fighting something in our bodies, which can just be a cold. You can get some over-the-counter decongestant for infants to help clear it up. If it's late at night or very cold outside, put us in a bath with menthol baby wash.

Here is the great experience of a menthol bath. First, make sure the bathroom door is shut to keep the warm air inside. Add the menthol wash while you are drawing our bath. Give us at least fifteen minutes in our bath and watch how many yuckies come running out of our nose! This is also breaking up phlegm in our chests. Once we are in the menthol bath that you have lovingly prepared for us, run a vaporizer in the bathroom. Put vapor drops in the vaporizer. The vaporizer will run at the same time as we are taking our vapor bath, creating a menthol steam. We affectionately refer to this as 'the menthol baby spa'. All the bad, yucky stuff just comes pouring out from our noses. It is okay to do this several times a day, but we recommend a 'menthol spa' be given before we go to bed so we can all sleep better. We cannot let this go without giving you the information you may need, in case we are having a really bad cold.

If we have a cough, we will start to 'cough-up' some of the phlegm in our lungs, as well. After we have a big cough finishing our bath, listen to our breathing. If we are making a wheezing sound while we are breathing, take us straight to the doctor. This could be a sign of an infection in our lungs. Of course remember to never leave us alone in the bath.

If we start to pull on our ears and are also upset while we are doing it, call our doctor. This is our way of telling you we may have an ear infection. Sometimes the fever does not come right away, but call the doctor especially if we are tugging on our ear and are running a fever.

With fevers not running over 103 degrees, you can give us some fever-reducer medicine or a cool bath, and keep checking our temperature throughout the day. Do double check with our doctor as to the right dosage we should have. It is very easy to overdose an infant with medicine. Sometimes we will run a fever just for twenty-four hours because our bodies are fighting a little something. It is possible there are no other symptoms and the fever is gone by the next day. With these types of occurrences, it is very likely that we just want to be held the whole day because of the internal discomfort we are having. On these days, we really appreciate your patience and love.

This is a time where we can only recommend you trust your 'instincts'. If we appear to be 'off' to you, please call our doctor. It is perfectly okay to call our doctors at anytime with any questions you may have. Here we have given you some simple suggestions of what you can do at home to help make all of our lives a little easier. If nothing else, these suggestions can help us sleep better through the night or out of some discomfort.

To bring this month to a close, we have one more suggestion to pass your way. This is a great time to show us picture books or baby books with lots of color and thicker pages. We can learn to turn the pages with you. (It also helps with our fine motor skills.) We will start to turn the pages, even if it is five at a time, which is great! Point to the pictures and tell us what they are. Do this with us each day. We will learn the images and colors, as they stimulate our imaginations and increase our language development. Thank you so much for doing all of this 'work' with us. We love you so much! You guys are the greatest!

Chapter 10

The Eighth Month

"Hi!" we say, as we learn to wave to you! At the least, we are trying to. When you help us wave 'Hello' or 'Good-bye', we are learning to wave, greet and give a salutation. It is never too early to learn the basic manners; we would rather please than displease you and your company.

Wow, eight months old! Now, though we have told you that the development schedule is not exactly the same for every baby, most of us fall into a two-month window of variance for development.

We are going to tell you about some developmental achievements that you should be able to observe. If we are not able to do these particular things, you will need to contact our pediatrician and see if there may be some exercises that you can do to help us. A physical therapist who specializes in infant development could help us out. By eight months, we should be able to roll from back to front and from front to back. We should also be able to pull our knees up underneath us and rock back and forth. We should have good control of our head and be able to sit up. If we are unable to do these simple movements, please inform our doctor. This can indicate for some reason, our gross muscles are not developing in the manner that they should. This is why we keep trying to express why 'tummy time' is so important.

This includes us spending time on the floor ourselves and with you while you do your exercises, so we may model your movements. It is extremely important our 'core' muscles are developing properly. They are truly the 'core' of who we are. Our core muscles are what help us to stand and sit up, pull our legs under us to crawl and hold our head up high.

This walks us right into another life-learning lesson: holding your head up high helps to alleviate depression. Teach us from the very beginning to stand up straight and hold our heads high, for all the years you will support us as parents and other important people. (This is good information for you, too. Take note that if you are ever feeling bad and putting your head down because you cannot face the world, hold your head up!) Remember that we learn from MODELING YOUR BEHAVIOR! If you do not keep your head up and smile, we will learn to put our head down, too. Teach us to embrace life and have the confidence to take it on! We love you! As we will mimic your smile, laughter, babble and 'happy days', we will also mimic your tears. Your fears will become our fears. Instead, run through life laughing and playing, and so will we. Love life as you love us...unconditionally!

Do not be surprised if some of us are trying to pull up on furniture or anything else we can get our hands on, including you! Again, be aware of our movements. If we are becoming more mobile, remove any and all objects in our path that could cause us harm. Also, remove all momentos you would not want us to get our hands on, and could break. We would never want to hurt your feelings like that.

Let's have a little chit-chat! We are getting some good 'baby chatter' and 'babble' down by now. You will even be to understand some of that, too. Isn't that cool? Language and communication development is imperative for us to interact with the world.

Since we are eight months old, we will mention some

sensory developmental steps that should be observed by now. We should respond to a loud noise we are not expecting, usually this response is noticed by us making a sudden movement. To test this without damaging our hearing, stand behind us, about eight feet away and do a single loud clap. If we jump or try turning our heads to see if we can find the noise source, that is good. Try saying our name if we do not respond to the clap, or singing a nursery rhyme we should know, to see if we respond. Make sure that you are standing behind us while performing these tests and the area is not full of noise. If we are not responding to these sounds, call our doctor to have a hearing test done.

Just a note, do not stamp your foot as a way to make a loud noise. If we do have a hearing impairment, we will feel the vibration of your stomp through the floor and turn to see where it is coming from. This could give a 'false-positive' on our homemade hearing test. Please, do not be discouraged if we have a form of hearing impairment. If you haven't noticed yet, we have learned to be able to communicate our needs and wants to you without having a conversation.

To check both our hearing and vocal sounds at the same time, place us directly in front of you. (We have actually been doing these things already, it's just that now you know why they are even more important to do, other than looking so cute.) Move your mouth and make a sound like, “Aaaaahhhhh”. We should follow your mouth movement and then repeat that sound back to you. Next, try an, “Oooohhhh”. Again, we should try to repeat the sound back to you, or at least you can tell that we are trying to mimic your sound. This is another way to check our development on language and communication.

Verbal communication takes much longer to build than physical communication, sign language, or ‘body language’. Cross your arms over your chest. This means ‘love’; an embrace and a hug. Blow us a kiss with a smile. We love you, too. Of course, if we are within reach, go ahead and give us that hug and kiss. Give us lots of them! You can never share too many. Love is a language that needs no words. Physical contact and interaction will solidify that feeling. You can still say, “I love you”, twenty times a day for it is never too much!

We cannot express enough the importance of communication with you. The many types of communication will carry us through our lives. The information in this chapter, like the others before, have guides, hints and very important information that impact our lives now, as infants, and throughout the rest of our years.

Communication, begins on day one, and is critical for a happy and healthy life. In this book we are giving you ideas in how to be able to spend time with us and the importance of bonding. Knowing that you are going to take time for 'just us' is a special moment to look forward to everyday. As we get older, we will grow with confidence knowing you are there for us each day. Most parents want to raise strong, confident children and turn them into equally strong, confident, and loving adults. These are YOUR baby steps! We are taking our baby steps in development, but know this is the doorway to the rest of our lives and you are the ones who hold the key.

What a great experience life is! We thank you so much for all the time you have taken to make sure that we are growing up well. Wow, it seems as though these eight months have been going by so quickly. Can you believe we are twice our birth weight? Some of us have tripled our birth size. A good average could be that we have grown about four inches and have gained five to seven pounds since our arrival. Of course, this is an average, not an exact. Our pediatricians have growth charts they use to measure us by during our well visits. This information is documented each time we go in to see the doctor.

The most important thing during our first year is that we are consistently growing in length and gaining weight. At the very least, we should gain weight each visit. Some of us who are lighter at birth (i.e. five pounds) and are breast-fed this whole time can gain one pound each month! Those of us who were bigger from the start (i.e. seven to nine pounds) may gain about six ounces each month. Again, these are just guidelines but we should maintain being within our healthy boundaries. Babies should have 'baby fat'. We should have good weight all over. This includes 'healthy amounts of fat' on our faces, hands, arms, legs, bottoms and feet. Make sure that our weight is proportionate to our height measured by our growth chart; if we are twenty-five inches long and weigh twenty-five pounds, we are overweight and if we are twenty-five inches long and weigh only ten pounds, we are underweight. Do not stress if this is not always the case as we are still individuals and grow in our own ways. It is just important to try to maintain a healthy lifestyle. We should consistently have a good balance of weight.

This is why we explain each month when food is introduced that it is not to take the place of our breast milk/formula feedings. These feedings are still the main reasons for stimulating our growth to include brain and bone development and muscle strength to help us moving in the right direction. Cereal, snacks, and jars of food, are to be *in addition to* these feedings. Still note if we push our spoon, bottle, or breast away, we are full. Let us digest, thank you.

Chapter 11

The Ninth Month

It is so hard to believe in eighteen months we have done a 180-degree turn. Nine months ago, we were just being born. But, nine months before that, we were just barely a thought. (Until you took that test, then went into a panic and called everybody you knew.... Well, you know what happened.) Either way, all of this was only eighteen months ago. A year and a half! Whoa! After that, there was growing in your womb, getting shoved out, and landing on the planet. Then we learned how to swallow, suck on a nipple, use a spoon, sing a nursery rhyme, smile, pass gas, roll over, push up, understand our hands, and learning to talk without knowing any words.....! We believe we are truly amazing individuals thus far. We shall give a moment of silence while we listen to you clap loudly for all of our crowning achievements. (Take as much time as you need, it's okay. Here's a tissue for those who are shedding a few tears. Thank you very much for all of your support. We love you all.)

Thank you so much for your wonderful applause. And we would like to address your achievements briefly, as well! Let's see, you have taken us on thirty travel days, changed 1897 diapers, made 2012 bottles, (for breast-feeding moms; dry, cracked nipples, bitten twice, engorged breasts 24 times, and 1 dry milk duct), 1904 burping lessons, 212 nursery rhymes sung, and have clapped your hands 10,456 times. Whew! Well done! Bravo! Stupendous! And all of those other wonderful words! Way to go!

How many of us are now trying to pull up on furniture or other items? Looks like it is about 30%. If we are not doing this, that is perfectly okay. We are not behind at all. How many of us are trying to dress ourselves? (By 'dress ourselves', we mean we are helping to push our arms through our sleeves, looking as though we know what we are doing.) Okay, the show of hands on that is about 75%. This is good. This does not mean we will be dressing ourselves in a month, but we are trying to help.

This is a good time to start making a 'play clothes' box.

We are calling it a 'play clothes' box because some big people get confused into thinking that 'dress-up' refers to girls only. This is NOT true in any way. Girls and boys, equally will try to put on mom's heeled shoes, accessorized with a purse, some sort of a big necklace, and topped with dad's briefcase.

Here's a hint, dressing up in *any way, shape, or form* does not determine what kind of adults we will be, except for the use of creativity, patience, and expression of how much we love you. Enjoy this. This is about the time where you will be able to see us want to play with these items (and this will continue for years). As we get older, we will add more costumes to our box and of course, take some away. Always check the box periodically to make sure that there are not any broken items or objects that could be a choking hazard. Also at nine months, we cannot do the 'dressing up' all on our own, this is fun to do together or with a group. A 'group' can even be our parents, brothers, sisters, cousins, aunts, uncles, and grandparents, too. Get as many different hats as you can because they are so neat to play with. Playing dress-up in front of the mirror is great so we can see how we look. We will be playing with our 'play-clothes' box for a long time. On the side of germs, wash our play-clothes from time to time and in addition, a spritz of an antibacterial spray in our box from time to time won't hurt. Thank you for making us one.

Here we are toppling over once again. It won't be long until we actually can use all of our muscles at the same time for one purpose. Until that time, we understand it is fun to watch us figure it out. We also hear you laugh. We are trying hard to laugh with you, too, even if it is directed at us. Laughter is always the best medicine! It is so cool to know this information.

Wait, here comes.... another good lifelong lesson. As we are trying to figure out how to use all of our muscles, we tumble, fall, sit up and have 'oopsies'. If we fall over and start to cry, let us know we are okay; give us a hug and a kiss or distract us with laughter. We are not exactly sure how to articulate the emotions we are feeling at the exact moment of our accident. Most of the time we are just fearful of what just happened more than anything else. This is exactly when we look to you to see how you respond. If you rush over to us screaming and are very upset, we will be very upset, too. Part of this is what we learn from you, that even a little 'oopsie' is something to be afraid of.

Having a constant fear of being hurt or just knowing

that you will scream, can keep us from trying anything new. This can adapt into a dependence that is not healthy as it takes away the part of us that wants to experience life. This is really not a good thing for either of us. Instead, if we have an 'oopsie' and begin to get upset, just come over and ask if we are okay. Look us over for any 'boo-boos' that we may have acquired and give them a kiss to make them all better, or a little tickle can work. Truly, kisses are amazing in their healing powers. We will learn the difference between an 'boo-boo' and a real injury.

If we have a real injury requiring medical attention, try to remain calm while calling our doctor. Going to the doctor or an emergency room right after an injury, can be pretty scary for us. It is not our warm, loving house. We look to you to help us remain calm. If we need to have medical attention, bring our favorite stuffed animal, book or blanket to help us stay as comfortable as possible. As with everything else, if you do not know if our 'boo-boo' is in need of medical attention, call our pediatrician. As a benefit ti being more calm, you can accurately answer all of the doctor's questions to the best of your ability. It is always better to be safe than sorry.

We are addressing emergencies more in this month.

We are coming into our own with our mobility that will only increase from here. We are just mentioning a couple of hints to help all of us along. If we receive a head injury and a big, nasty, scary bump appears, this is usually a GOOD sign! As horrible as it may look, it is much better that the swelling comes to the surface rather than swelling on the inside, which can be more life threatening. Try to put ice in a cloth on the bump or swollen area, or even a cold wash cloth. (A bag of frozen peas will work.) This will help bring down the swelling. Check to make sure our eyes can follow your finger moving back and forth in front of us and are following the same path of direction equally. You are looking for one eye going in a different direction; this can be a sign of a concussion and we should seek immediate medical attention.

Some 'boo-boos' look very scary and are actually just a small cut after being cleaned up. Sometimes we fall flat on our face and our 'new' teeth cut our lip. The scary part is when you pick us up and there is blood in our mouth and on our teeth, lips and gums. This is a horrific vision. Stay calm, grab a wet wash cloth and wipe away all the blood that you see. This is how you can determine where the injury is located and what kind of injury it is. We know mouth, face, and head wounds can be very frightening. Please try to remain calm and find the source of the injury. If you do this and feel the injury requires medical attention, you are better equipped with accurate information to give to the nurse or doctor. You will be able to let them know where the injury is, how it looks, and what it is doing. Here are some descriptive phrases: 'the wound is swelling', 'has been bleeding steadily', 'it is swollen and bleeding', or 'there is an object protruding from the body'. An object protruding could be a small piece of glass, rock or splinter. A piece of glass (or another object) that you do not want to remove on your own is bigger than the size of a splinter, have someone from a medical background remove it. (These are highly unfortunate and unlikely situations and we cringe explaining them to you.) We cannot stress enough how incredibly important it is that you remain as calm as possible. We will now more likely stay relaxed while you tend to our needs and find out all the information you need to assess the situation.

Thank you so much for all of your time and patience. We can get really scared, but we look to you first for your calm reaction. We also look for you to smile, after you have checked us all out. After everything, give us a kiss and hug and let us know we will be okay. We believe in you. Remember that kisses have big healing powers and sometimes that is all we need. We have come to find out that kisses really are magical.

Well, now that we have gotten that scary part taken care of, let's move on to some other attributes associated with this month. We should be sleeping more this month. We could be sleeping eight hours easily, have a feeding, then go back to sleep for another two hours. It is funny, moms and dads, we will sleep longer when you are not around. Yes, it is like we know when you are there. We love to be around you and have all of your attention. It is just true that we will be more awake and more demanding in your presence. We will wake up early from a nap if we know you have just arrived. It is because we love you so much and want as much attention as we can get.

By the ninth month, hopefully, we have tried a good assortment of baby food. Some food items we initially gave a bad face to at some point, would be great to have us try again now. We may be more accepting if you give us a little time to work full circle around our 'new' foods. As stated before, we absolutely eat more than three meals a day. This is still *in addition* to our formula/breast milk feedings. We should be having at least six of these a day. If you are feeding us a good hearty lunch, followed up by a bottle or breast-feeding, this will usually bring us to our midday nap. Our nap should be about two hours or so. We will still be sleeping about 15 hours out of a 24 hour period.

You know the cool thing about being nine months old, other than our highly acclaimed talents? How much smarter we are. Our senses and brain synapses are becoming intertwined. For example, if you go behind the couch, we crawl over to where we last saw you. We do this now instead of crying because we believe you had left us. Our eyes are watching you walk to another room and our ears are hearing that you are still talking. We are puttin one and one together and are figuring out that you are just on the other side of the wall. What a relief! We finally put that together. This is a great time to play 'peek-a-boo' and get the true cause and effect of playing it.

If you haven't noticed yet, we are dropping items on the floor. Yes, you will pick them up and give them back to us. Contrary to popular belief, we are not doing it just to watch you pick them up (though it is amusing). You see, when it leaves our line of sight, we believe it is gone. All of a sudden, you bring it back and it is there again. That is amazing. To us, we begin to learn things that disappear can come back. In an odd way, it is similar to attachment. If we never experience something leaving and coming right back, we may not trust it will, or that you will. If we see you go around the corner and can still hear you, we trust you will come back. If you ever have to leave, try not to make it too long or often. Another lifelong lesson we will trust is knowing you will come back to us.

We are trying to learn about attachment. Outings for our 'big people' a few times a week, are good. We exist and you exist, yet we know that you are always there for us and will be returning to us. It is funny how dropping a toy over and over again off of our highchair tray can have so much meaning. That is exactly why we are writing this book.

Well, a 180 degree turn; how do you feel, kid? Oh, yes, we know we are the baby, but we trust that you know the next years will be a little easier to take if sometimes you can be a kid, too. Remember, you are doing wonderful and we truly love you.

Chapter 12

Ten Months!

Hey there, good looking! We are in the double-digits now! Wow! Sorry about the whole baby weight thing; you know, the weight *you* gained? Hopefully, that is all gone by now. It is just a small price to pay for bringing one of us into the world (hee, hee, hee). Yeah we can laugh now, we know, (but we understand that the 'baby weight' will come back to us in some way, shape or form). We do love and appreciate all the extra cushion you gave us. We know you loved having all those extra chocolate fudge sundaes in the middle of the night, but look where we are now!

This is a good month to develop a bit of a change in our sleeping habits. Most of us are still waking up in the middle of the night for a feeding. If you would like to, you can start phasing that out. Most of us will wake up for about five minutes, if that, then fall back asleep. As we said, try to phase it out. We know and love the fact that you are waiting to hear our cries at night for our feeding. Soon you will relax and be able to sleep the night away, too! We can sleep for about eight to ten hours before waking for a feeding, a diaper change, and then go back to sleep. We are still sleeping an average of 15 hours in a day, but the duration is definitely longer than seven months ago. How great this change is! We hope you are making sure you are getting the adequate rest you need. Just a hint, if you need help with things, even around the house, just ask. (Well, not us...) Somebody who could help prepare a meal, vacuum a room, or do the dishes. Believe us, people understand. For some, it helps to have us in one of those back or front carriers while you accomplish these tasks. Just know that everthing begins on a higher note when you are well rested.

We hope you receive that information well. Not any one person can do it all. Okay, so back to us! Our mobility is becoming better and strong now! It is wonderful to see us crawling around. Some of us are doing the 'full-on crawl', some of us may prefer 'the army-crawl', and some do the 'one leg crawl-and-scoot'. If we are doing any of the above mentioned move-abouts, great! Some of these look funny, too, but are perfectly normal.

Though it is an amazing thing, some of us may be trying to really stand up and 'furniture walk'. These are huge, funny, and scary steps for us. This is how it goes - we pull ourselves up and then, "Woah, woah!" Our butt goes out and comes back in. Okay, let's try to keep the butt more in. We think we got it. Now here go the hands. Left hand let go, let go.....open the fingers...see how that is working. All right, now what? Look at how great it is that we opened our hand..uh-oh, woah, hold on to something again, now! Whew! That was close! Okay, now that we've got our hand back down, let's scoot over. Pick up this leg; wow, that was easy. Look how strong we are! Okay, now put it back down. There we go! Try to keep the butt in - all right! Yeah! We did it! That is how we 'furniture crawl'! We did it! We did it! Shake your butt, shake your butt, shaky, shaky, shake your butt. Whoops, don't fall. Good job, us! We hope you got that on camera (kind of). It is more for your entertainment than ours, but we only learn this once. When we learn to walk really well, then run, this entertaining stuff won't happen again. As we already know you do enjoy watching. We are happy to put a smile on your face.

"Mama", "Dada", "Gaga", "Ba-ba" - we are saying all of

these words on purpose! We are smiling at you while you walk in the door or when we crawl into the bathroom and push that big door open! Ta-da! We then sit up proudly since we just pushed open that great big thing. Now we will sit on our bottoms and do a shaky, shaky dance. We are so cool! Who does not just love us! Our kisses usually have a big wet slop attached with them, but we are trying to show how much we love you!

"Aaaaaaaaahhhhhhhhhhhh!" Did you hear that? If you didn't, you must have not been in the house because that was so loud. That was cool! We so did that on purpose and enjoyed every minute of it! If you question this, just notice the big huge smile on our face after we have performed such a lovely note. Just smile and laugh with us! It is strictly up to you if you feel like recording this, but we would give fair warning to individuals before watching (for volume purposes).

Bath time is so much fun now. We can sit up, but it is still highly recommended that we are kept in a smaller bath tub. Some mommies and daddies still put us in the kitchen sink and some still have us in a 4-in-1 bath tub of some sort. This is good because we may be able to sit up, but we could easily fall or roll over into the bath water where we could choke or drown. Please make sure you are staying right with us while we are bathing since we can drown in one-half-inch of water or less.

It is so neat to us now that we can splash in the water and play with some bath toys! The water sure does go everywhere while we are playing. This is great! (We do recommend in these very fun and wet bathing events you wear clothes that are okay to get wet. Just like at the amusement parks, the sign reads, “You will get wet on this ride!”) We are very much laughing with you while we are enjoying this experience (another good time to catch on film - standing further back of course). We do apologize for the occasional ‘peeing’ episode. The one that occurs when we first go into the bath and you then have to take us out, rinse the tub, and do it again. It’s just that sometimes a warm, fuzzy feeling comes over us which sets off a urinating trail!

Thank you for all of the nursery rhymes you have been singing and acting out with us. We are learning how to do so much of them with you. It is just like when you start to sing, “Twinkle, twinkle, little star,” and we try to say “star”. Also, when you put your hands above your heads to make the ‘twinkle, twinkle’, we try to do to copy you! This so much fun and we would not be able to do it without you! Thank you for all of your hard work; it is truly a blessing besides that we are establishing a wonderful relationship between us and all of you. Please, tell us your life stories, no matter who you are, teach us to understand your wisdom and experience so that we willlearn to appreciate others as everyone has something unique to bring into each other's lives. Life is so amazing, isn't it? Thank you for making ours as full as possible!

Chapter 13

Eleven Months Old!

Wow! It is so hard to believe we will soon be a one-year-old! This has been one heck of an adventure, wouldn't you say? We believe you agree. How are our table manners? Are you impressed? No? That's okay, we are just excited that we are getting our spoon to our mouth. Applesauce is a yummy dessert after dinner, followed by our bottle or breast-feeding. This is the life! Bath time is so much fun, crawling gets us where we want to be quickly, and pulling up and trying to stand while we shake our bootie is the best ever! We have adjusted to having the middle of the night feeding taken out, so you are getting a better night's sleep, just like us! Somebody was telling us that we will just get older and learn more stuff, like cleaning our room? What is that about? We are perfectly fine where we are now. And who would blame us?

We are fed when we need it, which is regularly. We can still go potty in our diaper and someone changes it. (Hopefully, sooner rather than later if we have done a 'number two' because that scent doesn't leave our surroundings.) Plus, we can get a nasty diaper rash and that isn't good either. We do appreciate your diligent effort on that part. Anyway, stinky stuff aside, we are doing our nursery rhymes and we can turn pages in a book. We also point at pictures and say simple words that you understand. We say a whole lot more words that only we understand and that's okay, too. We are also bathed in hugs and kisses everyday! (Hint, if this is not happening, it should be.) What a life we lead! We can only be forever thankful to you for all of these wonderful things.

Now since we are moving about so much, our kick-gym may not be as useful. Some kick-gyms can change into pull-up tables or ball-dropping twirls, and this would be a good time to change it. Age-appropriate toys are very important; that's why toys that change and grow with us are wonderful to have. You see, if we have toys that are too young for us, then they are not challenging. If there are toys that are too advanced, then we will get confused and frustrated and walk away. There are still some toys that will not bore us, though make sure the size of the toy is appropriate. Balls, blocks, and large-stackable toys are great because we constantly grow with them. See if we can line blocks up together, then if we can stack them up high, at least six blocks high. At the same time as we are either lining them up or stacking them, count with us and tell us the colors. Repetition, repetition, repetition is how we learn.

Here's another idea, get some jumbo size crayons and teach us how to color! Show us how to hold a crayon, not eat it, and to make lines and circles. We will start to copy what you are doing on paper or in a coloring book, right along with you. (Here's a clue, washable crayons are so much easier to clean if we miss the paper or use the wall as our canvas; hence, the 'washable' part. Also, make sure that the crayons are 'nontoxic'.) Get a big piece of paper and draw a flower (anyone can make a flower, it doesn't have to be perfect) and watch us sit next to you and try to make one, too. Don't say anything, just draw and watch how we follow you. Isn't that just beautiful?

Speaking of other items that are beautiful, let's look at our smile. So, now that we have teeth, we need to make sure that we have changed how we clean our teeth. It is still helpful to wipe our gums and teeth down, sure. We need to move on to using a toothbrush. Most companies have beginner toothbrushes listed as 'Stage 1' or 'Infant Brush' size. The bristles are very soft and the head of the toothbrush is small, to fit our size of mouth. Please, do not use one of your toothbrushes on us as it is just too big and hard. Also, make sure that you use 'Infant' or 'Beginner' toothpaste. This type of toothpaste is 'fluoride free', which is okay to swallow. 'Big People' toothpaste has fluoride and you do spit it out after brushing and we will not learn to spit anytime soon. So to be on the safe side, get the flouride-free toothpaste. Hopefully, you have done what we asked and are not leaving bottles of milk, breast-milk or juice in our mouth when we go to sleep. It is not good to rot our teeth just as we are getting them. As long as you have followed these simple guidelines, we will be smiling beautifully.

There is another subject that we have not touched on yet and we feel that it is very important that WE tell you about it. Now that we are eleven months old, we are becoming very mobile. Some 'big people' have started to introduce a list of rules, suggestions or demands. This is a silly thing to do. We are just figuring out shapes, sizes, colors and things that rattle and roll. To believe that you give us rules and that we will obey them, as though we understand every word you say, is just a disappointment waiting to happen.

Follow this scenario to see how this works. We are moving around our house just as we told you we would do, and we come to the shelf under the coffee table. There is a magazine on the shelf. We pull the magazine out from the shelf, drool on it, look at it and eventually it starts to make an interesting noise while it is coming apart in our hands. A big person enters the room and says, “Mommy told you not to do that”. Okay, so what were we not supposed to do?

We understand ‘Mommy’; that’s you. You look a little upset, we are not receiving hugs and kisses, so maybe it is something that just happened. Now, is it the crawling part? Don’t think so. Is it touching the shelf, or pulling the magazine, or drooling, or that noise before the magazine made two pieces? Then the big people wonder why we just stare at them. Maybe we do not understand your words and we just don’t get it. It took a few actions before the ‘upset look’ appeared. That is too much information for us to digest. We still lick the food we don’t like because we do not remember that we don’t like it. Even though our brain is growing at an astronomical rate since our beginning days, we just don’t have a good memory yet. So, this is why we will clue you in to having a 'baby-fied home'.

'Baby-proofing' your home is much different than making it 'baby-fied'. Baby-proofing consists of making sure that all sharp or harmful objects are taken out of our reach. Also, use covers for the electrical sockets, rubber corners on sharp corner tables, and keep the crib's stuffed animals to one or two. This is how you 'baby-proof' the house.

Now, to make the house 'baby-fied', put magazines out that you have already used on the coffee table or bookcase; these should be magazines that we can look through and it is okay if they get ripped. Fill the bottom two shelves of the bookcase with our cardboard books. If we can reach the shelf above that, put a 'textured toy' in front of your books, or a mirrored soft block. You see, a reflective block will distract us from our desired destination as soon as we see it. A good 'textured toy' can be a snake where each part of the toy has a different feel and makes a different sound. Now, if we reach for one of your books and touch the textured toy and hear its sound, it will distract us before we reach your book. There are two reasons for this; one, we do not have long-term memory, thus creating number two, we are easily distracted. Just as you can distract us when we are upset or deter us from something harmful. In essence, a 'baby-fied' home is one in which we are enticed to learn without being prevented from moving in every direction. We truly hope that we are also not being confined to a playpen all day because we cannot learn a lot in there.

A 'baby-fied' home is also one where we are welcome to explore and grow. Our muscle strength increases because we are free to roam and we are constantly stretching our muscles and trying to do more. We are pulling ourselves up, standing, crawling, and maybe even walking! This is difficult to do in a confined space or while being kept in a 'bouncy' chair. Bouncy chairs or playpens are good to use if you are mopping or vacuuming, or have to use the bathroom, but not for any long period of time. Another benefit that most big people do not realize is what moving in all directions does to us on the inside. We are more willing to try new things and our confidence increases, as well as our sense of awareness. We do more problem-solving activities such as rolling a ball, then following the ball to see where it goes. There is nothing better than this. Here we are free to explore, in a safe environment, where we can try almost anything from playing with a ball, to reading a book, to shaking a rattle.

If there are stairs that we can get to, please put a baby

gate up, leaving the rest of the area free for us to roam in. Always be right there with us if we attempt to crawl up, or down, the stairs. We also know that, at the same time, if anything happens, you are there. Thank you for giving us the best home in the world to grow and be nurtured in.

Chapter 14

Twelve Months Old!

Here it is, the grand finale! We are twelve months old! And boy, do we have a lot to go over. We may have to actually take a nap in the middle of this, so please bear with us. Where to begin? With our muscles, or shots, colors, facial acknowledgments, or talking? Well, there is a good bit to cover, so let's just begin. First, let us thank you with all of our hearts for really listening to us and all of our needs. It is difficult sometimes to communicate everything, but you have done a wonderful job. We would also like to thank all of the supporting cast in helping you get through this first year. For those of us who have older siblings, thank you for helping to teach us the things you know, plus the extra kisses you gave us when the 'big people' weren't looking. Smooches right back at you! Thank you to mommy, daddy, grandma, grandpa, aunts, uncles, baby sitters and family friends who came over to help cook or clean or watch us for a 'special night out'. You have been wonderful in your support. We are simply amazed by how many people are around us to help us grow. We cannot thank you enough for all of your hard work. Bless you, from the bottom of our hearts. Kisses and hugs all around; it's on the house!

Okay, now that we have given our 'thank you' speech, we still have to go over a few things. Let's start with the mirror. As we explained earlier, the mirror is a wonderful place to learn a great many things. At twelve months, we should be able to recognize five body parts - any body parts. Of course, the more we know, the better. It is okay if we cannot say them all, but at least we can acknowledge them. For instance you say, "nose", and we point to our nose, then cheeks or feet or hands. We know you understand now. It is important that we know this at twelve months, touching base on intellect and recognition, with the use our fine and gross motor skills.

As we just stated, we may not be talking a lot, but hopefully we are saying some recognizable words, such as 'mama', 'dada', 'juice', 'baba'. If we are saying 'mommy' and 'daddy', it is wonderful that we have learned to enunciate, showing that we are increasing our language and communication skills. If we are crying most of the day, every day, this is a warning sign that there is something wrong that we are not able to communicate to you. Make a journal of our daily routine if this is happening during our day. Bring the journal to our doctor to see if they have some suggestions to help on make our days better.

Let's move on to food and feeding. If you are still a breast-feeding mother and wish to continue to do so, please do. There is still no better form of milk for us with all of the extra vitamins and nutrients that we receive. For most of us, after our first birthday, it is okay to start us on whole milk. Double-check with our doctor if it is appropriate at this time to give us whole milk. The fat in the milk helps keep a 'healthy' weight on us but, most importantly, the fat nourishes our brain while it is still developing at such a rapid rate. During the first twenty-four months of our life, we experience the highest brain growth and activity in our entire life span. It is so very important that you keep this in mind. Until we are introduced to milk, and if we are not breast fed, continue using formula in our bottle.

Rolling into another 'twelve month-ism', buy a double-handled juice cup for us to sip our juice from and have with us at meal times. This a good time to introduce some table food. Pay attention to exactly how many teeth we do have and what food we can chew. It's good to ask the doctor for a list, in case you do not know. Steak, for instance, is not a good idea. If you want to try spaghetti, good. Use a little bit of sauce, not too spicy, to get the noodles wet. But, cut the noodles into 3/4 inch pieces. (Here's a hint, at spaghetti time, just take our shirt off. It is easier to clean our bellies than to scrub out tomato sauce). Meatloaf, that isn't too spicy, can also be cut up into small enough pieces that will be easy for us to chew. Mashed potatoes, mashed sweet potatoes, broken soft bread rolls, pieces of cheese, or pieces of cheese pizza are good to try.

When you are introducing new items like this, don't leave us alone, in case we choke. Hot dogs are still considered a choking hazard, even when they are sliced. However, if you take the round cut slices and cut those slices into four quarters, they are much less of a choking hazard. Cooked 'cut green beans' are easy to pick up and eat and are very good for us, too.

We can also have increased variey of snacks, like a couple of crackers with a few quarters of sliced cheese. We can snack on toasted oat cereal, which we love, or any cereal without added sugar that is circle-shaped with holes. (The shape of this cereal is to keep you mindful of potential choking hazards.) Most makers of infant food products have growing lines of food items for us. Some items are tiny raviolis or very small cooked peas and carrots. A raw carrot would be too difficult for us to eat. Some of us have 'gummed' on them while we were teething, but we are not ready to eat them just yet. Yogurt is great to feed us and some of us have oatmeal (not too hot!). There are also very healthy fruit and vegetable snacks made by our wonderful baby food producers. Once we put these snacks in our mouth, they start to melt. This makes it less likely for us to have a choking spell. Eggs are something else that you do not want to introduce to us until after our first birthday, just like peanut butter. The main reason for this is because of potential allergic reactions.

Just as we explained before, new foods and liquids are introduced separately with some time in between to watch for allergic reactions. Make sure that we always have a very well-balanced diet of protein, calcium, fruits, vegetables, and grains. Yes, we do still have lifelong lessons left to tell you. Keeping a well-balanced diet will keep us from becoming neither underweight nor overweight. Being either underweight or overweight can produce life-threatening issues that would be best for us all to avoid. Believe us, we just got here and we want to enjoy every minute of it.

Guess what follows diet? Wow, you are good. It is exercise. Going back to the 'fourth month' chapter, we introduced pilates or yoga for you to do, along with some wonderful floor time for us, to establish a beneficial pattern of exercising. We bring up exercising again just because they are very important. If this activity was bumped out of our schedule, you will realize the wonderful impact that it has on our lives and try to find a way to work it back in. This is for both of us, as you know, and it builds into, wait, another lifelong opportunity. If exercising with us becomes your routine, we will not having any problem wanting to exercise on our own. Also if we, or you, are having a bad day, this is a healthy way to work it out. The other cool part, when you register us for peewee soccer or tee-ball or tumbling, you do not need to find time to practice with us because it is already in the schedule! Thus, this is great for both of us for a long time. Thank you for all the fun workouts!

Now, although we have said that development varies for each of us, all of us should be able to roll from back-to-front and front-to back. We should all be crawling in some way, shape, or form. We should be trying to pull ourselves up on objects or people and trying to take steps. We should all be able to sit up and hold our head up with control. Some of us even sit for twenty minutes before losing interest and wanting to go somewhere else. We should be able to throw a ball overhand. We should be able to stack seven blocks on top of each other and line up seven blocks next to each other on the floor. With all of these tasks, we are using our gross motor skills and fine motor skills with balance and control, testing just how much we have developed against a standard measurement of growth.

Try this test with us. Draw a line on a piece of paper and see if we can draw our own line on the paper with yours. If so, great! If not, then we need more work on that skill. It doesn't have to be at all perfect, but the line just has to show that we are trying to follow your pattern. Next, is a circle. It is perfectly okay if we make a lot more circles than you do, as long as we try to make the circle. Starting from one point and going around to come back to meet that point. We should be able to follow a line with movement. We should also be able to recognize some simple pictures like a bear, cat, dog, or cow. It is good to show us a page that has a couple of items on it before you ask us, "Can you show me the bear?" Then, we point out the bear to you on the page and try to say the word. Great! Next, using the book, see if we can turn the pages on our own. It is okay if we grab a few at a time as long as we are understanding the concept of page-turning. It is so wonderful that you have read to us and pointed out pictures so that we will be able to recognize them and learn to turn the pages, too!

Since we have been using our shape sorter for months now, shapes are easy for us. We should be able to point out a square, triangle, and circle. We should also be able to recognize four colors: red, blue, green, and yellow. If we know more colors than this, that is wonderful! Applause for both of us!

We believe that we are all still in diapers. Just because our first birthday is coming up, that does not mean that we are ready for potty training. If we are forced into potty training before we understand how our bladder works, this can cause future problems with being able to control our bladder and bowel movements. We can most definitely wet the bed for years, and have many accidents, if we are forced into toilet training before we are ready. Not only will we not be able to determine when our bladder is full, our bladder will not know when it is full, or when it is time to release, because our brains did not have time to figure it out. So, please, do not force potty training on us at this young age; it will become much more work for you than the diaper changes you have to do now. On the positive side, we should be using fewer diapers. We can't really say less stinky, but fewer, yes.

On the average, most of us at twelve months have increased our weight by two-and-a-half times our birth weight. If our weight is much more or less than this, refer back to the exercise and feeding area of our book. As long as we gain some weight each month, that is a good sign of growth. We have also gotten much taller than we were at birth, as much as six inches. We hope you took a lot of pictures because we won't shrink back to that small size again. (Keep the camera handy for our first birthday cake; those photos will become classics!)

We were distracted by cake momentarily, but we are back in full force now. We did not state in which month we were to have a well visit and our immunization shots because pediatricians, health clinics, and the health department may follow different schedules. However, we truly believe that you found somewhere to take us to have all of our immunizations, so that we have stayed current with our shots and have not lapsed. Immunizations help to get us through life, literally. They are mandatory for most preschools, schools and day care facilities. One thing is certain: there is a standard list of immunizations we should have by the twelfth month of life.

We are going to list them in order:

1st shot - Hepatitis B

2nd shot - Hepatitis B

3rd shots - DTaP, Hib, Polio

4th shots - DTaP, Hib, Polio

5th shots - DTaP, Hib, Hepatitis B

At twelve months, we will receive an MMR, Hib, Polio and Chicken Pox vaccine. Sometimes the doctors will combine the immunizations to minimize having to give individual shots, thus diminishing the number of painful shots for us. (Thank you, Doctor DoRight, for teaching that part of the class, we will never forget you!) You will be happy to know that if we have all of these shots by twelve months, we will only receive one more DTaP shot at fifteen months. We won't be required to get any more immunizations until right before we start kindergarten. Oh yeah, and we will enjoy the ice cream or special treat you get to distract us when that time comes.

Please note that, even though we are becoming more independent, mobile, and confident, some days we may not like people, especially people we haven't met before or seen in a while. Do not be upset that at twelve months old, we may not go willingly to someone we don't know. They may have good intentions, but we don't know them and will likely throw a fit if you just hand us over to them. We are not doing it to be rude, but they are strangers to us. To clear up the whole mess, just set us down and you guys come on down to our level. If we are then comfortable to go over we will, but it will be on our terms of comfort and trust. Thanks for your understanding.

It has been wonderful to share all of these experiences with you. We can't thank you enough for your time and patience for taking the time to read our book. We are extremely appreciative of each loving and caring 'big person' who took the time to come down to our 'babyhood'! Our life has blossomed in these first twelve months, yet this is just the beginning. We truly believe that we have given you valuable information that will help you feel that you are a great parent each day.

How wonderful it is that we don't spit up on you anymore, too! (That was just a little mess to clean, sorry about that.) Instead, we can smile and laugh and play with you. We can roll a ball back and forth with you. Now, maybe we cannot catch a ball yet, but we are working on a pretty good throw. This has been a wonderful experience so far, but we are ready to have our cake and eat it, too!

So, without further ado....Happy First Birthday to us, Happy First Birthday to us, Happy First Birthday to all of us beautiful babies.... Happy First Birthday to us!! Yeah! See you next year!

With all the love in the world, from your babies!

Letter to All Our Mommies and Daddies

Dear All of our Mommies and Daddies,

Because of you, we were blessed with life. You have been here for a while now and have learned so much more than we will ever know, except for the love of family. The bond between parent and child is a love that only an eternity can measure. We do not know about bills, insurance, phone calls, cleaning, and a forty-hour work week. We do know that the true meaning of life is that we have life for as long as we do. Share in our life with us, especially if life is trying to teach you a lesson.

Every day we do smell the roses, bask in the sunshine, and snuggle in your warm embrace. Play with us, dance with us, and dream with us. Do not ignore us or harm us in any way for this can cause pain for many years to come.

Teach us how to apologize by apologizing to us if you have done us wrong. We will forgive you. Use good manners with us so we will learn good manners. Please, do not try to put each other down in our presence. If you happen to do so, apologize to each other, also in our presence. Do not take us aside to say something bad about the other parent, thinking that we will love you more; that will never work.

When you travel, take us with you. Show us the world and all that it has to offer. Teach us that everyone is equally beautiful, no matter how different they may look; they have children around them, too. Life is too short to hate. First embrace life, then grow with it, and finally, be thankful for it. Without life, where would we be? Just remember that every step you take, three little ones are being taken right next to you. We may not say anything, but we see everything. Be with us because, for us, you will always be kings and queens. We will always love you more than you will ever know.

From your sons and daughters,

XOXO

Additional Resources

As you may know, we are not doctors, so we did additional research for some of our topics to make sure that we would not harm any babies with the information that we have given.

Please, feel free to look over these sites yourself for additional information.

American Academy of Pediatrics

www.aap.org - Health and well-being of infants and children, information on circumcision

North Carolina Healthy Start

www.nchealthystart.com - Development, play and shots info

Federal Department of Agriculture

www.fda.gov - benefits of breast-feeding

Dr. Greene

www.drgreene.com - wonderful pediatric info, many topics

Pampers Parent Stages

www.parentstages.com - parenting info & baby development

Canadian Parents

www.canadianparents.com - advice & chat for parents-to-be

Zero To Three

www.zerotothree.org - parent & infant info, public policy info to help better the lives of all infants & children in the USA

Early Head Start National Resource Center

www.ehsnrc.org - With ‘Zero to Three’ info on infants development & bonding; help for parents with limited income in the USA